Mountains, Rivers, and the Great Earth

SUNY series in Environmental Philosophy and Ethics
J. Baird Callicott and John van Buren, editors

Mountains, Rivers, and the Great Earth

Reading Gary Snyder and Dōgen in an Age of Ecological Crisis

Jason M. Wirth

Cover image courtesy of Nathan Wirth.

Published by State University of New York Press, Albany

© 2017 State University of New York

All rights reserved

Printed in the United States of America

No part of this book may be used or reproduced in any manner whatsoever without written permission. No part of this book may be stored in a retrieval system or transmitted in any form or by any means including electronic, electrostatic, magnetic tape, mechanical, photocopying, recording, or otherwise without the prior permission in writing of the publisher.

For information, contact State University of New York Press, Albany, NY
www.sunypress.edu
Production, Jenn Bennett
Marketing, Anne M. Valentine

Library of Congress Cataloging-in-Publication Data
Names: Wirth, Jason M., 1963– author.
Title: Mountains, rivers, and the great earth : reading Gary Snyder and Dōgen in an age of ecological crisis / by Jason M. Wirth.
Description: Albany : State University of New York Press, 2017. | Series: SUNY series in environmental philosophy and ethics | Includes bibliographical references and index.
Identifiers: LCCN 2016031502 (print) | LCCN 2016050289 (ebook) |
  ISBN 9781438465432 (hardcover : alk. paper) | ISBN 97814384-65425 (pbk) |
  ISBN 9781438465449 (e-book)
Subjects: LCSH: Snyder, Gary, 1930—Criticism and interpretation. |Dōgen, 1200–1253—Criticism and interpretation. | Ecocriticism.
Classification: LCC PS3569.N88 Z965 2017 (print) | LCC PS3569.N88 (ebook) |
  DDC 811/.54—dc23
LC record available at https://lccn.loc.gov/2016031502

10 9 8 7 6 5 4 3 2 1

山河大地
[*senga daichi*—mountains, rivers, great earth]

Here, everywhere, right now is mountains, river, and earth.
—Dōgen, "*Baika* [Plum Blossoms]" (S, 585)

The mountains, rivers, and the great earth are all the ocean of buddha nature.
—Dōgen, "*Busshō* [Buddha Nature]" (S, 238)

Clear and bright are mountains, rivers, and earth—an eyeball.
—Dōgen, "*Ganzei* [Eyeball]" (S, 616)

Ancient masters [Yangshan and Guishan] said to each other, "What is the wondrous clear mind?" "I say it is mountains, rivers, and the earth; it is the sun, the moon, and stars."
—Dōgen, "*Sokushin Zebutsu* [The Mind Itself is Buddha]" (S, 46)

When you move mountains, rivers, and earth, as well as the sun, the moon, and stars to practice, they in turn move you to practice. This is not the open eye of just one time, but the vital eye of all times.
—Dōgen, "*Shoaku Makusa* [Refrain from Unwholesome Action]" (S, 97)

Saying that the self returns to the self is not contradicted by saying that the self is mountains, rivers, and the great earth.
—Dōgen, "*Keisei Sanshoku* [Valley Sounds, Mountain Colors]" (S, 89)

Avalokiteśvaras . . . all work together with buddhas, mountains, rivers, and earth.
—Dōgen, "Avalokiteśvara" (S, 403)

Walking on walking,
 under foot   earth turns.
Streams and mountains never stay the same.
—Gary Snyder (MR, 9, 145–146, 154)

    great
    earth
    saṅgha
—Gary Snyder ("O Waters," TI, 73)

For Elizabeth Myōen Sikes,
embodiment of the emptiness of the three wheels:
giver, receiver, and gift

Contents

Acknowledgments ix

Abbreviations xi

Preface (Milarepa's Stone Tower) xiii

Part I The Great Earth

1. Mountains, Rivers, and the Great Earth 3
2. Geology (Poetic Word) 25

Part II Turtle Island

3. Place (Land and Sea, Earth and Sky) 57
4. Bears (The Many Palaces of the Earth) 71

Part III Earth Democracy

5. The Great Potlatch 87
6. Seeds of Earth Democracy 103

Notes 117

Bibliography 133

Index 143

Acknowledgments

I would like first of all to thank Gary Snyder who, despite the countless demands upon his schedule, made the time to read this manuscript and to offer generous words of encouragement and support. I would also like to extend my whole-hearted gratitude to my brother Nathan Wirth, whose photography is a great inspiration and teacher; to my Dharma brother Carl Kakuzen Mountain who early on read the manuscript and shared his wisdom with me; to my Sōtō Zen teacher Kōshō Itagaki, abbot of the Eishoji Zen training and practice facility in South Seattle; to my beloved Dharma sisters and brothers of CoZen, especially Brian Shūdō Schroeder, Bret Kanpū Davis, and Erin Jien McCarthy; to my companions at PACT (The Pacific Association for the Continental Tradition), especially Gerard Kuperus, Marjolein Oele, Tim Freeman, Chris Lauer, and Brian Treanor, all of whom have offered much support and guidance on this project; to my companions at CCPC (The Comparative and Continental Philosophy Circle), especially David Jones, Michael Schwartz, and Andrew Whitehead, all of whom teach me both with their wisdom and their friendship; to my friend Josh Hayes, whose own work on Gary Snyder has been instructive; to the poet Samuel Green, who teaches me with both word and deed from his home on Waldron Island; to the incomparable Bill Porter (Red Pine); to the many members of the Seattle University EcoSangha; to my friends Don Castro and Mark Unno, who manifest the Pure Land in deed and word; to Andrew Kenyon, my thoughtful and gracious acquisitions editor; and to my former students and current friends Jennifer Luo, Caity Orellana, Maura McCreight, Sonya Ekstrom, Emily Ingram, Brigid Scannell, Lia Perroud, and Dominique Walmsley. Finally, I would like to thank my wife, Elizabeth Myōen Sikes, the great alchemist who turns each day of our life together into gold.

Some parts of the first chapter appeared in a much different and shorter form as "Painting Mountains and Rivers: Gary Snyder, Dōgen, and the Elemental Sutra of the Wild," *Research in Phenomenology*, vol. 44 (2014), 240–261. Some parts of the second chapter appeared in a much different form in "Never Paint What Cannot Be Painted: Master Dōgen and the Zen of the Brush," *Diaphany: A Journal & Nocturne*, volume 1, ed. Aaron Cheak, Sabrina dalla Valle, and Jennifer Zahrt (Auckland and Seattle: Rubedo Press, 2015), 38–65.

> Hard to stack wood & live
> in the moment. The body knows
> the picking & spacing & wedging
> to make the stack right. The mind is in
> December by a good fire, soup
> simmering on the back of the stove, coffee dark
> as winter nights, & the sound
> of a six-day rain on tarps
> over the woodpile.
>   —Samuel Green, one of a series of "Small Noticings,"
>   *All That Might Be Done* (Pittsburgh: Carnegie Mellon
>   Press, 2014), 52.

(Used with the author's permission)

Abbreviations

AH *Axe Handles.* San Francisco: North Point Press, 1983.

BF *Back on the Fire: Essays.* Emeryville, CA: Shoemaker & Hoard, 2007.

DP *Danger on Peaks: Poems.* Emeryville, CA: Shoemaker & Hoard, 2004.

EHH *Earth House Hold: Technical Notes and Queries to Fellow Dharma Revolutionaries.* New York: New Directions, 1969.

GC *The Great Clod: Notes and Memoirs on Nature and History in East Asia.* Berkeley: Counterpoint, 2016.

GSR *The Gary Snyder Reader: Prose, Poetry and Translations, 1952–1998.* Washington, DC: Counterpoint, 1999.

HWH *He Who Hunted Birds in His Father's Village: The Dimensions of a Haida Myth* (1951). Emeryville, CA: Shoemaker & Hoard, 2007.

LR *Left Out in the Rain: New Poems 1947–1985.* San Francisco: North Point Press, 1986.

MHM "Mountains Hidden in Mountains: Dōgen-zenji and the Mind of Ecology." In: *Dōgen Zen and Its Relevance for Our Time.* Edited by Shōhaku OKUMURA. San Francisco: Sōtō Zen Buddhism International Center, 2003.

MR *Mountains and Rivers without End.* Washington, DC: Counterpoint, 1996.

NH (in conversation with Julia Martin). *Nobody Home: Writing, Buddhism, and Living in Places.* San Antonio, TX: Trinity University Press, 2014.

OW *The Old Ways: Six Essays.* San Francisco: City Lights, 1977.

PM *This Present Moment: New Poems.* Berkeley: Counterpoint, 2015.

PS *A Place in Space: Ethics, Aesthetics, and Watersheds: New and Selected Prose*. Washington, DC: Counterpoint, 1995.

PW *The Practice of the Wild* (1990). Berkeley: Counterpoint, 2010.

RW *The Real Work: Interviews & Talks 1964–1979*. Edited by William Scott McLean. New York: New Directions, 1980.

S Dōgen's *Shōbōgenzō*: *Treasury of the True Dharma Eye*. Edited by Kazuaki TANAHASHI. Boston and London: Shambhala, 2010.

TI *Turtle Island*. New York: New Directions, 1974.

Preface
(Milarepa's Stone Tower)

> I became a poet that I might give voice to the songs I heard in nature and my inner ear, and that also, by the power of song, I might contribute to the downfall of the technological-industrial world, its total destruction, in favor of a world based on closer knowledge of nature in man himself.
> —Gary Snyder in 1970[1]

I

This is a book about reading Gary Snyder (b. 1930) and, to a lesser extent, the great Kamakura period Zen Master Eihei Dōgen (1200–1253),[2] during the ongoing ecological crisis, what Snyder has called "this time of New World Disorder" (BF, 25). Every poem may have its "Twentieth of January" as the great Romanian poet Paul Celan insisted, in his case referring to the date of the Wannsee Conference that resulted in the Final Solution. Our Twentieth of January—and Gary Snyder's Twentieth of January—is our rapidly accelerating and explosive war against the Great Earth.[3] For this reason, this is not a general study of either Snyder or Dōgen. I do not attempt to chart the development of their respective ideas or to elaborate every facet of their thinking and writing. This is rather a meditation and philosophical engagement that seeks to read, think, and practice *along with* both of them in a manner that is mindful of the place from where one reads them today. It seeks to express something of *the place from which* Snyder and Dōgen practice, think, and write. In this sense, this is also a book from and about the Dharma.

Plenty of good books have already been written on both Snyder and Dōgen, respectively. Although this study embraces the scholarly and has gratefully and indispensably benefited from it, it is not my intention just to add to the stockpile of scholarship. I hope also to attend, for want of a better word, to the *spiritual* dimension of both what Dōgen called the Great Earth and our prevailing ecological crisis. This spiritual dimension is currently endangered, that is, it is becoming harder and harder even to appreciate the spiritual as a problem or question. The spiritual seems increasingly irrelevant to anything that matters, but given our current sorrowful state of human habitation, never has it been more urgent.

I confess some distaste for the word *spiritual*. It has become so broadly applied so as to mean little, if anything; it has a long and philosophically dubious history, a history that often reinforces the kind of thinking that I am trying to get beyond; it often proposes an otherworldly perspective when the problem is that we have not been present to the earth;[4] it often vaguely expresses a dissatisfaction with the prevailing institutional forms of religion, while hoping, somehow, some way, to satiate the needs that traditional religion seems to have betrayed; and it is often a disavowal of the rigor and intelligence, as well as the compassion and the wisdom, that the current ecological crisis demands. I use this word cautiously and temporarily as a sort of down payment on a more nuanced manner of speaking to this dimension of the problem: the current crisis is not so much a failure of rationality, but a symptom of *the poverty of our practice*. We—and by that I mean both humans and the earth with its myriad forms of shared life—*are as good as our practice*.

In the face of our folly and stinginess, practice is the cultivation of wisdom and compassion within our interdependent becoming with, through, and, in some way, *as* all other forms of life.[5] Or as Snyder translates the famous opening line of the *Dao De Jing*: "The way that can be followed ('wayed') is not the constant way," which for Snyder says: "A path that can be followed is not a *spiritual* path" (PW, 161). Snyder calls this the path that cannot be followed—because it is not in the end a path at all—the "wilderness. There is a 'going' but no goer, no destination, only the whole field" (PW, 162). Zen "turns you inward rather than giving you a rule book to live by" (RW, 153). It is the hope of the present book to make this sensibility clear and to show how it matters.

II

The news about the human relationship to the Earth continues to be dim and often feels like it is growing ever dimmer. As I write these words, I feel the weight of some of this year's bad ecological news: 2015 has completely shattered the record (2014) for the warmest year officially recorded; we have learned that ExxonMobil, one of the most profitable enterprises in the history of enterprise, knew for decades of the "catastrophic" externalities of its business model, but considered them acceptable; indeed, they invested millions of dollars in confusing a generally gullible public about the science that they personally knew was true.[6] Meanwhile, rather than having sober public discussions about these kinds of events, Donald Trump—the archetype of the American huckster—gluttonously consumes the media's attention, proffering an alarming program of racism, xenophobia, misogyny, thuggish violence, rabid militarism, and capitalist voracity. Unsurprisingly, he dismisses climate change as a hoax. It is with mourning as deep and sorrowful as the sudden death of a loved one that as this book enters the world, Trump assumes the presidency. This book is my unrepentant defiance.

During the last energy crisis in the early 1970s, Snyder argued that everybody "thought it was money that counted before. Now it turns out that the only real wealth is oil" (RW, 51). That either oil or money would count as wealth is a symptom of profound *spiritual* poverty, a clear indication of ruinous practice and poor etiquette. The desire to acquire obscenely large amounts of things (fossil fuels, money, consumer goods, power, fame, etc.) is endless. As Snyder quotes Gandhi: "For greed, all of nature is insufficient" (BF, 35). More is never enough. The nub of our spiritual poverty is that we think that the massive accumulation of goods counts as wealth. For Snyder, the "actual 'real wealth' is knowing how to get along 'without' . . . 'Do more with less,' as the slogan goes" (RW, 51).

The ecological crisis therefore brings us to a great crossroad. "This is a marvelous time in which the nations of the world may get a new balance and a perspective on themselves—if it doesn't degenerate into hysteria and short range crisis thinking" (RW, 51). Never has there been a better time for "creative people, poets, religious people" to speak (RW, 51). Yet the challenges only seem to grow deeper and more daunting and short-range crisis thinking has so far generally prevailed. It is a time of war, not just against each other, but also more deeply against the imagination and creativity as well as the earth. "What is happening now to nature worldwide, to plant life and wildlife, in ocean, grassland, forest, savannah, and desert in all spaces and habitat can be likened to a war against nature" (BF, 62). Although poor treatment of the Earth is not new, its magnitude—its elevation to a condition of total war— seems unprecedented.

Tellingly, nowhere in the current bizarre media carnival can one find due attention being paid to the ongoing Sixth Great Extinction event. Regardless of how one comes down on the science supporting the nature and extent of this event, the ongoing onslaught on biodiversity is undeniable and its ravages are grievous and mournful. As Snyder reflects in *The Practice of the Wild*, extinction is not the problem that we kill our fellow creatures—death belongs to the way of all life; it is rather an assault on *natality*, the elimination of lineages of birth that have evolved over billions of years.

> The extinction of a species, each one a pilgrim of four billion years of evolution, is an irreversible loss. The ending of the lines of so many creatures with whom we have travelled this far is an occasion of profound sorrow and grief. Death can be accepted and to some degree transformed. But the loss of lineages and all their future young is not something to accept. It must be rigorously and intelligently resisted. (PW, 188)

Ecosystems and the myriad life forms they sustain will likely eventually recover from the onslaught of our contemporary mode of being, but it will take many millions of years to replenish biodiversity to its preindustrial levels. "Hundreds of millions of years might elapse before the equivalent of a whale or an elephant is seen again, if ever" (PW, 188). The devastation of biodiversity since the end of World War II has been especially explosive. Furthermore, the loss of an individual species is not just a loss of that species, but a wound to the ecosystem of which it was once an integral part. "It isn't just a case of unique lineages but the lives of overall ecosystems (a larger sort of almost-organism) that are at stake" (PW, 188). The Buddhist teaching of *anitya* or nonpermanence is not resignation to and indifference about the destruction of life. Because all life has life without owning life, because to *be* is to *be contingently and interdependently*, and because birth and death—(*shōji* or *saṃsāra*)—are inseparable, "all the more reason to move gently and cause less harm" (PW, 188).

The crisis nonetheless continues to accelerate. The best time to act was in the 1970s when Snyder and many others were asking us to do so; with each year of inaction, counteraction or, at best, insanely insufficient action, we dig ourselves and our companion creatures deeper in a hole. It is in this context that I think of the following words, written by Snyder more than four decades ago:

> A war against the earth.
> When its done there'll be
>   no place
> A Coyote could hide. (TI, 23)

Of course, we should not flatter ourselves that the survival of the Earth depends on our actions. Despite its human inflicted wounds against biodiversity and the systems that foster it, it will survive us, although it is not presently clear that we will survive ourselves. Snyder has a clear sense of the "dark" side of the Wild and both he and this book reject any kind of New Age fantasy about an original, pristine, harmonious Wild. This is not a call to somehow become "one" with nature. Both the fossil record and the existence of fossil fuels testify to the earth's capacity to undergo unimaginable ruin. There is ample evidence that in the extreme long view, the earth and biodiversity ultimately profit from the earth's catastrophic, game-changing events. We need only remember that the current crisis has been preceded by five other extinction events, including the almost unfathomable scale of the demise of the great reptiles. Although the image of nature as in an abiding steady state ignores the geological record of catastrophe, there tends to be very long periods between such cataclysmic alterations, which contributes to the inductive fallacy of a permanent homeostatic system. This may never have been true, but the climate emergency dramatically reverses this assumption: tipping points and rapid change are becoming normal events. Nonetheless, our unhinged relationship to the earth is a question of etiquette, of ethics, of finding a more sacred manner of wayfaring, of clear-eyed compassion for who and where we are.

III

Gary Snyder is one of our Elders:[7] a Zen teacher and shaman poet[8] with his ear to the ground of the West Coast of Turtle Island, including its indigenous stories, and who inspires as much by practicing another mode of dwelling on earth as he does by his powerful poetic-philosophical-scientific articulation of it. His poetic craft stems from the underlying mindfulness that sustains it (NH, 86). In a way he continues to write as Chōfū, "Listen to the Wind" or "Listen, Wind," the Dharma name given him by his teacher ODA Sessō Rōshi.[9] I do not mean this is in any literal sense; in Zen discourse, what matters is not just what you say (although that, too, is very important), but also the manner in which what you say allows you to show your mind, to exhibit your manner of consciousness. "It's how you contact the basics and the base of yourself" (RW, 83).

Snyder told Gene Fowler in 1964 that there is not a strictly conscious reason why he holds the "most archaic values on earth," including "the fertility of the soil, the magic of animals, the power-vision of solitude, the terrifying initiation and rebirth, the love and ecstasy of the dance, the common work of the tribe." They are not derived from books—as necessary as study is—but they are "in the Buddhist sense, rooted in the belly; and this is where the breath starts, so where the poem starts" (RW, 3). The center or ground of Zen practice is not found in the cogitations of the scholarly mind but in the *hara*, the abdominal center of one's breathing. In Zazen, we do not so much escape thinking, that is, imagine that it can be merely negated and then disappear, but rather strive to get at the seat of thinking, which is not found within thinking itself.

Dōgen famously distinguished in his very first writing, "*Fukanzazengi* [Universally Recommended Instructions for Zazen]," between what is sometimes translated as "nonthinking" (*hi-shiryō*) and the mere negation of thinking, namely, *fushiryō* or not-thinking. If the *fu* is acting as a privation or negation of thinking (*shiryō*), then the "non" (*hi*) is not negating thinking but rather pointing beyond or even beneath thinking.[10] It is to begin consciousness, including thinking, at its root in the *hara*. In a way, it is also, as Snyder put it in 1976, to "de-educate" oneself, to practice a complementary deep unlearning, to fathom Linji's "true person of no rank" or what Snyder called your "*original mind* before any books were put into it, or before any language was invented" (RW, 65).[11]

Although it is always true that one must go into the singular depths of one's own practice and *hara* in Zazen, it is not the case that practice is therefore merely an individual quest or concern. No one can practice for you. You must enter it yourself and not rely on secondhand experiences; "the best priests of the kiva are the ones who are able to show you the path out the door where there isn't any lore" (RW, 65). Just as no one can die your death, no one can do your practice. Nonetheless, practice not only clarifies the mind and opens the heart, but in so doing it takes one beyond oneself into the shared webs of all life, dependent co-origination (*pratītyasamutpāda*), or what Chinese Huayan (or Japanese Kegon and Korean Hwaeom), following the *Avataṃsaka Sūtra*, revered as Indra's net. As Francis H. Cook articulated this "cosmic ecology":

> . . . since the net itself is infinite in dimension, the jewels are infinite in number. There hang the jewels, glittering "like" stars in the first magnitude, a wonderful sight to behold. If we now arbitrarily select one of these jewels for inspection and look closely at it, we will discover that in its polished surface there are reflected *all* the other

jewels in the net, infinite in number. . . . This relationship is said to be one of simultaneous *mutual identity* and *mutual inter-causality*.[12]

It begins with the first step of the Noble Eightfold Path, namely, right view [*dṛṣṭi*] (RW, 108), which is the dawning of wisdom [*prajñā*]. Although this perspective still goes largely against the grain of our age, to deem it therefore impractical or hopelessly idealistic is to be prejudiced by the ideology of our age. What Snyder's living and writing pursues "are essentially sanities even though they appear irrelevant, impossible, behind us, ahead of us, or right now. 'Right now' is an illusion, too" (RW, 112). The "right now" is based on all manner of unsustainable practices and delusions (e.g., that capitalist growth is possible ad infinitum, that all growth is equally valuable simply because it is growth, that the earth has an endless supply of fossil fuels and raw materials, that populations can grow as much as they desire, that technology can overcome any unintended consequences along the path of unending growth, and that we can continue to plunder the earth without diminishing ourselves).[13]

One does not necessarily have to designate seeing through the illusion of right now as an experience of awakening (*satori* or *kenshō*), although in our contemporary context, an awakening that is merely personal and private and that ignores the globalized economic and political web that shapes and threatens the very possibility of human life, is just another form of somnolence. Awakening is not the attainment of a higher plain of consciousness that condescends to the earth. It is not the resignation that just lets "things happen: you play an active part, which means making choices, running risks, and karmically dirtying your hands to some extent" (RW, 106–107). Regardless of what it takes to see through the ordinary madness of business as usual, Snyder attributes his capacity to do so to his Zen practice. As he humbly told Doug Flaherty in 1969:

> I don't lay claim to any great enlightenment experiences or anything like that, but I have had a very moving, profound perception a few times that everything was alive (the basic perception of animism) and that on one level there is no hierarchy of qualities in life—that the life of a stone or a weed is as completely beautiful and authentic, wise and valuable as the life of, say, an Einstein. And that Einstein and the weed know this; hence the preciousness of mice and weeds.[14]

Although a scientific ecology and what Cook has called a "cosmic ecology" are clearly related, they are not the same. The latter amplifies the former, opening up a different relationship to oneself and the Great Earth. In both Snyder's poetry and the interrelated four teachings of nonself (*anātman*), emptiness (*śūnyatā*), nonpermanence (*anitya*), and dependent co-origination (*pratītyasamutpāda*), the insights of scientific ecology matter in new and more consequential ways: "imagination, intuition, vision clarify them, manifest them in certain ways" (RW, 35), decentering the human and opening her in compassion to the value of all things, no longer as things, but as living expressions of the Buddha. Hence, "the best things in life are not things" (MR, 152). David Landis Barnhill writes that "in effect" Snyder has "ecologized" *pratītyasamutpāda*, allowing it to absorb and benefit from all of the critical work that scientific ecology has accomplished, while simultaneously having "'Buddhacized' the notion of ecosystem."[15] Or as Snyder articulates the insight in a Buddhist sūtra:

> The Buddha once said, bhikshus, if you can understand this blade of rice, you can understand the laws of interdependence and origination. If you can understand the laws of interdependence and origination, you can understand the Dharma. If you understand the Dharma, you know the Buddha. (RW, 35)

In this sense, ecology is not only a question of knowledge—although that aspect remains indispensible—but of wisdom. And wisdom is not just a question of knowing, but of knowing in an open, affirmative, compassionate manner. Not ecology as scientific knowledge of how beings interrelate, but a love of the Great Earth, just as it is, in its suchness (*tathātā*). "What are we going to do with this planet? It's a problem of love; not the humanistic love of the West—but a love that extends to animals, rocks, dirt, all of it. Without this love, we can end, even without war, with an uninhabitable place" (RW, 4).

The ecological crisis is also a question of systems, ones that, as the Marxists and post-Marxists and Critical Theory philosophers have long recognized, coopt practice into the pernicious ecologies of capitalism and other modes of global dominance. In an increasingly globalized world, an insidious version of *pratītyasamutpāda* also manifests. Capitalist ideology has globally captured almost everyone in its web; the challenge is to reimagine our archaic communion with the Great Earth anew.[16] "My small contribution to radical dialectic is to extend it to animals, plants: indeed, to the whole of life" (RW, 130). This is what Snyder called "the Mind of the Commons" (PW, 39). One can no longer act without the whole web of life in mind. Buddhist right livelihood (or any kind of religious virtue) is no longer simply a question of individual accomplishment and responsibility. To assume that it is cedes too much to global ideology. These are "abnormal times" and "we just have to keep as clear a head as possible and steer away from the worst of it. But everybody's involved in it" (RW, 88).[17]

Moreover, it is not even true that human selfishness and stinginess benefits human beings at the cost of all other beings. From the perspective of *pratītyasamutpāda*, stinginess is in the end also extremely self-destructive. Our self-interest drives us to actions that in the long run betray the self-interest that fostered them. For example, in pursuing wealth at all costs, we destroy the air, water, and food chain that enable us to live and be healthy. This cycle has now become harmful on a staggering scale. The starting point for an etiquette of living that addresses the pernicious effect that we have not only on our supposedly individual selves, but also on the creatures with whom we share our being is therefore an earth awakening, a deep transformation of human consciousness. This is also the Buddha Way with its own practices of earth awakening foregrounded. While the crisis is systemic—Buddhist interdependence teaches us that we are also only as good as the relations that comprise us—it is also "spiritual" (a question of practice).

Although the various competing religions and spiritual practices do not all strive after the same thing—it is not all just one big religion—and although some strands of religious and/or spiritual practices may no longer be defensible, one does not have to become a Buddhist in order to be in one's own way a bodhisattva (awakened being) reborn to the Great Earth. Pope Francis and his remarkable encyclical *Laudato Si*[18] are a case in point. The Vatican—or at least Pope Francis—has come a long way from someone like Pope Boniface VIII who in 1302 declared in a papal bull that "it is absolutely necessary for salvation that every human creature be subject to the Roman Pontiff." For Francis, "rather than a problem to be solved, the world is a joyful mystery to be contemplated with gladness and praise" (LS, 11–12). The humiliation of human life for the benefit of a few and the degradation of the earth—our common good—betrays it; it knows no gratitude, failing not only to acknowledge the gift of each and every moment of life, but to declare such grace a treasure and to vow that one is always on the side of the earth. Francis memorably cites Pope Benedict: "The external deserts in the world are growing, because the internal deserts have become so vast" (LS, 158). Who are we? "We are its problem species" Snyder tell us (BF, 24). The Great Earth is showing us who we are!

This sister now cries out to us because of the harm we have inflicted on her by our irresponsible use and abuse of the goods with which God has endowed her. We have come to see ourselves as her lords and masters, entitled to plunder her at will. The violence present in our hearts, wounded by sin, is also reflected in the symptoms of sickness evident in the soil, in the water, in the air and in all forms of life. This is why the earth herself, burdened and laid waste, is among the most abandoned and maltreated of our poor. . . . (LS, 3)

"For this reason," Francis tells us, "the ecological crisis is also a summons to profound interior conversion. It must be said that some committed and prayerful Christians, with the excuse of realism and pragmatism, tend to ridicule expressions of concern for the environment. Others are passive; they choose not to change their habits and thus become inconsistent. So what they all need is an 'ecological conversion'" (LS, 158–159). In the Buddha Way, we call this awakening. When we are verified by all things, that is, when we experience ourselves as belonging to the interpenetrating rhythms and ways of the earth itself, Dōgen tells us, we are awakening. However, when we seek to verify things and subject the earth entirely to our ways, that is delusion.[19]

The Buddha Way is also an ecological conversion that opens one to gratitude, and in such gratitude, one becomes mindful of the way of all beings. This is the Buddha Dharma version of Zosima's teaching to the young Alyosha Karamazov—when you awaken, you will know it because you will fall to the earth and water it with your tears of gratitude. One elemental practice is to bow to all things. Little cockroach, I vow to you, my little teacher. Even a mote of dust, Dōgen tells us, is enough to turn the Dharma wheel.

IV

The development of this book's line of thought travels along three interconnected paths.

It begins with a discussion of what Dōgen calls the Great Earth and what Snyder calls the Wild, comprised of the play of waters and mountains, emptiness and form. The discussion includes a consideration of what it might mean to address the Great Earth with painting, the poetic word, and sūtras. The language that addresses the Great Earth is composed of the same wild and elemental forces as the Great Earth itself. Both are in their own way what the

Mahāyāna tradition calls "skillful means [*upāya*]." A "true teaching has no particular shape" (S, 245) Dōgen tells us. "The entire phenomenal universe and the empty sky are not but a painting" (MR, epigram) as he also tells us.

From the Great Earth with no beings and places left out, I turn in the second part to a consideration of the place where this book was written, namely the West Coast of Turtle Island. I first discuss the problem of place and then turn to a discussion of bears and another way to think of place as one of the many palaces (or worlds) that coinhabit the Great Earth.

The final path consummates the discussion of the mutual implication of the Great Earth and Turtle Island through a discussion of earth democracy, a place-based sense of communion where all beings are interconnected and all beings matter. I first discuss this indirectly through an investigation of the "big potlatch we are all members of" (PW, 20) before turning to a consideration of the seeds whose maturation is the practice of earth democracy.

In my pursuit of these three interlocking paths, I am forswearing the traditional academic distance that confuses the rigor of careful thought with the spirit of abstraction and the academic professionalism that keeps the issue at hand at a safe distance. This book is its own intimate practice, its own attempt to awaken to earth democracy. It does not want to hide behind the ruse of academic jargon or the alienation of academic distance. I believe that the issues about which Snyder writes and the manner in which he writes about them really matter. I hope to pursue in my own way and to the best of my ability Snyder's devotion to "unmuddied language and good dreams" (TI, 94). I agree, as Snyder declared in "Is Nature Real?," that "we need to stay fresh, write clean prose, reject obscurity, and not intentionally exaggerate" (GSR, 389). It would be a travesty to pretend to illuminate Snyder's clear, direct writing with writing that delivers him back to the clutches of academic obscurity.

That being said, I would also like to reiterate my intention to write not so much *about* Snyder, as if he was some kind of curatorial object, *but rather along with him and from the place and quality of mind* out of which he practices, thinks, and writes. To hazard a metaphor, one could say that this book is a kind of colophon on the sūtra scrolls of Snyder's various and varied writings, and as such it is my effort to testify in my own way to how I think I have heard the depths speaking in Snyder's "real work." A colophon is written by later owners of a scroll in order to bear witness to and confirm the quality of mind being expressed by the scroll. It is intended to help complete a scroll painting, but not by obscuring or replacing it. It endeavors to enact in its own way a link in a chain of what we might here call Dharma communication or what Dōgen called "buddha to buddha [*yuibutsu yobutsu*]" communication. One attempts to testify to the depth of one's own understanding by appending one's own writing to the original work. It may be that the values that this present book espouses and explores, the values of a counterculture that challenges the somnolence of the master culture, have in recent decades, at least on Turtle Island, been "more clearly stated in poetry than any other medium" (RW, 166). Perhaps that is as it should be, but the new lines of transmission and new possibilities for clear and compassionate thought continue to find new fissures, new lines of flight, new openings to language, and that is what this present new colophon is intended to be.

As such I resist as much as I can one of the ecological disasters of academic life, namely, the monoculture of isolated disciplinary territories. We confuse the rigor of serious thought with hyperspecialization and become obtuse even to the breadth of our own disciplines, let alone to the full breadth of the life of the mind. This surrender to irrelevance to all but the few who share our narrow enthusiasms is a kind of auto-colonization of the mind—or at least it is evidence of our complicity, advertent or inadvertent, with our colonizers. The colonization of the mind usually proceeds by a "divide and conquer" strategy and soon each isolated intellectual monoculture becomes so exhausted from continuously reinventing the wheel that it has no time or energy to engage other thinkers across the disciplines.

This penchant for reinvention is far from "Marpa purifying Milarepa" (MR, 110) by telling him to build his stone tower, take it apart, and build it again "like each time was the first" (MR, 130). This kind of radical repetition— "always new, same stuff" (MR, 130)—eventually tore Milarepa from himself and delivered him to the Great Earth. Academic repetition is the opposite: it bespeaks our narrow-mindedness and insularity precisely at the moment in which the Earth is ever more violently demonstrating the folly of our ways. To extend the metaphor, I could say that I here endeavor to take apart Snyder's stone tower in order to rebuild it as I found it. In so doing, it is my hope that the Great Earth that sustains his writing also permeates the present study.

That being said, it is also true that we each come at the issue at hand from our strengths. My strength and training is in philosophy, but I recognize that this is no excuse to forgo becoming conversant to the best of my ability with science, the arts, anthropology, politics, indigenous issues, and other relevant modes of disclosure. It is my hope that this book is philosophy engaged not only in the requisite interdisciplinary dialogue but that it is also an exercise of philosophy engaging and performing what Snyder, "in the spirit of pagan play," dubbed "pan-humanism," that is, a "humanistic scholarship that embraces the non-human" (PS, 237). As we see in the concluding chapter, pan-humanism endeavors to extend personhood to all forms of life, indeed, to being and its myriad beings as such.

Pan-humanism stems from a "continuing 'revolution of consciousness' which will be won not by guns but by seizing the key images, myths, archetypes, eschatologies, and ecstasies so that life won't seem worth living unless one's on the transforming energy's side" (TI, 101). This includes a transformation of science and technology as well as finding one's place and digging into it (TI, 101). Real change is slow and it is not abundantly clear that we have enough time remaining. But, as the Buddha saw, unless we attend to the root of the problem, it is like a tree that grows back again and again because we just cut it off at its visible base. Until we attend to the problem at a sufficiently profound level, our would-be solutions are just further symptoms of the underlying problem. A somnolent mind is like having a piece of shit at the end of one's nose. No matter what it smells, where it goes, what it studies, what manner of politics it advocates, or whom it engages, it just smells shit. The first order of business is to learn to wipe that piece of shit off. If the mirror of the mind is not dusted, it only reflects a dusty world, no matter what it is given to reflect.

This cleaning and dusting of the archetypes and stories and symbols and dreams, to the extent that it is effective, is not felt for a long time. "Poetry effects change by fiddling with the archetypes and getting at people's dreams about a century before it actually effects historical change" (RW, 71). This book also hopes to do its little part in tinkering with the dreams of our time and place, dreaming of another mode of political appearance (earth democracy whose constituency is all of life and all that sustains life). When Snyder received the Numata Foundation's Cultural Service Award for the promotion of Buddhism in 1998, he was among a small number of Americans to do so and the only American poet to do so.[20] Snyder attributed this to his effort to push "ecological concerns toward the front of Buddhism," developing what has too often remained merely latent. He has done so "by asserting the rights of all beings, rather than a narrow ethic that applies only to human beings."[21] That ethics pertains not only to the land, as Aldo Leopold so adroitly discovered, but also to the great assembly of beings that comprises the dynamic interpenetrating webs of the Great Earth, may seem like a distant dream but we can no longer afford half-measures. "Nothing short of total transformation will do much good" (TI, 99).

Finally, this is a book that endeavors to find the fearlessness that Snyder learned from Zen and other practices and it is a book that issues from gratitude for the lightning bolt of awakening that is the *sanity* of his manner of wayfaring.[22] "Zen and Chinese poetry demonstrate that a truly creative person is more truly sane . . . I aspire to and admire a sanity from which . . . one has spare energy to go on to even more challenging—which is to say more spiritual and more deeply physical—things" (RW, 123). Of course, when insanity prevails, it is this kind of sanity that appears eccentric, unrealistic, crazy. What the great Elder Kongzi [Confucius] taught in the Axial Age seems even truer today: "As for Ning Wuzi, when the Dao prevailed in the land, he was wise; when it was without the Dao, he was stupid. Others might attain his level of wisdom, but none could match his stupidity."[23]

Except for wayfarers like Gary Snyder and Dōgen Zenji.

Tetsuzen Jason M. Wirth
City of Seattle and Ancestral Home of the Duwamish
Ish River Country, Cascadia, Turtle Island

PART I

The Great Earth

1

Mountains, Rivers, and the Great Earth

> *Here, everywhere, right now* is mountains, river, and earth.
> —Dōgen, *Baika* [Plum Blossoms] (S, 585)¹

I

Although his profile as a major American poet has been dramatically ascendant, Snyder's critical contribution to speaking in a compelling language, beyond the duality of art and science/philosophy, of our elemental relationship to the "great earth" (what he calls "the Wild" and, following Dōgen, the Chinese landscape tradition, and other Zen practitioners, "mountains, rivers, the great earth") is not generally appreciated. Snyder's work is sometimes pigeonholed as mere nature poetry with a twist of Zen mindfulness. David Perkins, for example, in his *A History of Modern Poetry: Modernism and After* (1987), includes Snyder in a group of poets like Robert Bly, James Wright, W. S. Merwin, and Galway Kinnell, who are discontent with the disappointments of "civilization" and who consequently seek its rapidly disappearing alternative.

> Oppressed by crowds and noise in cities, by roads, wires, and houses everywhere in the landscape, by the glut and litter of material goods, by daily reports of ecological pollution through oil spills, strip mines, smokestacks, and pesticides, by guilt at the extinction or near extinction of animal species, by terror of war, and by contemplation of the possible end of life on earth, the mind is tempted to turn against the civilization Western man has created.[2]

It is a familiar story: The Romantics sensed the looming disaster, but it has now arrived in its full fury. Allegedly trapped in "civilization," we long for its lost antithesis, "nature." Snyder becomes a neo-Romantic or a modern day

Rousseau nostalgic for a state of nature. Speaking of the Zen resonances in relationship to the poem "Trail Crew Camp at Bear Valley," Perkins observes that the poem's voice has been separated from the ego's voice and in this "abnegation of the ego" Snyder can exercise his "Zen ideal" by "concentrating on the immediately given." "Unity with nature or reality is to be achieved by being wholly where you are" (HMP, 587). While there is some truth in this kind of discourse (and its implication that in Snyder's poetry, it is the Great Earth itself that is somehow *speaking* is critically important), Perkins' analysis of all of these poets nonetheless reinforces the duality between nature and civilization that Snyder seeks to undo. Moreover, a return to nature, while perhaps nourishing and inspiring, could never be as serious as hard ecological science or rigorous ecological philosophy. This chapter is dedicated to dispelling this erroneous—and erroneously dualistic—view and to making a case for Snyder and Dōgen as Elders who belong to a long and complex set of lineages, ancient and contemporary, that span Western (Europe as well as Turtle Island's indigenous peoples) as well as Asian philosophical and poetic horizons. These are critical interlocutors in the emergence of an earth philosophy-poetics-ethics-science and the elemental language and language of the elements that allows us to be once again, in Nietzsche's celebrated phrase from *Zarathustra*, *faithful* [treu] *to the earth*.

I use this word *elemental* cautiously and in a very specific manner. When Doug Flaherty asked Snyder in 1969 if his poetry was elemental, Snyder resisted, claiming that the term is "not really precise enough for me. Everything is elemental" (RW, 20). He claimed, rather, that his work endeavored to be "myth making" or a "ritual and magic order against a pure song order" (RW, 20). As we see in the next chapter, the mythopoeic belongs to the art of *upāya* or Buddhist skillful means and the poetic word is not something that happens in a more elemental way than anything else. All beings are elemental. I use the term here in a provisional fashion to speak to the power of the poetic word to awaken in us an awareness that "everything is elemental" and to do so in a soteriological manner. The elemental speaks simultaneously of the Mountains and Rivers, form and emptiness, that is, the dependently co-originating elements of the Great Earth, as well of specific places, specific bioregions, indeed, of the singularity of particular ecological communities. The shamanistic magic of the poetic word seeks to call forth both the interdependence of being and the singularity of place nondualistically and transformatively. These are songs and myths that mindfully and ever anew expose the sacrality of the Great Earth, place by unique place.

In this sense Snyder's elemental earth language, rooted in Turtle Island,[3] and resonating with the Dao and *Mahāyāna* Buddha Dharma, is also nondualistic. Snyder and Dōgen help us to move beyond the following kinds of pernicious dualisms.

Ecology is a contemporary concern, not an ancient one. Dōgen's sūtra of the mountains, rivers, and the Great Earth, so thorough that not one inch of soil is left out, as well as Chinese landscape painting (*shan-shui*), are, as we see, a direct refutation of this claim. This is not to say that ecology meant the same thing and responded to the same challenges and context that it does today, or that Dōgen would have fully recognized such a word. Nonetheless reading Dōgen in this present moment exposes us to a sensibility that is already ancient in Dōgen's relationship to the Buddha ancestors. Such ancestors are much older than the official organization of practice into the myriad Buddha Dharma schools and lineages. Even Śākyamuni, the sage of the Śākya clan of Kapilavastu, is in some way a relative newcomer.

Ecology is a science, and only trivially a question of poetic production. Snyder, like Dōgen, breaks down the dualism between discourse and art and Snyder's own output, comprised of both essays and poems, exemplifies this nonduality and insists that it is rooted in the nonduality of the earth itself.

Human beings are in *an ecology or bioregion, and while dependent on it, they remain fundamentally distinct from it.* The human mind *is* an ecology, not *in* an ecology.

Western approaches to the problem are irreconcilable with Asian approaches. Snyder is rooted in both Greek and Asian lineages, as well as many others, including the ancient cultural veins of the Western part of Turtle Island. Who speaks for the West? Moreover, to the extent that one could say that science is a European contribution, it comes to a fuller expression of the Great Earth in its dance with Buddha Dharma. To oppose the "spiritual" and the "scientific" is to condemn the former to irrelevance and the latter to a flat, indifferent, and noncompassionate relationship to the marvels and problems that science contemplates.

Civilization is opposed to the Wild. This duality, in which we are all either uncritically absorbed in Heidegger's loathsome *Gestell* or Neo-Romantics pining for the missing woods is especially pernicious and also belongs to the heart of the prevailing ecological crisis. The fantasy of a return to pristine nature, untouched by fumbling and contaminating human hands, is destructive of both civilization, which imagines that it flourishes in opposition to the Great Earth, and the wild, which is being dominated and consumed to an unprecedented and unrestrained degree by contemporary imperial civilizations.

And finally: *The elements only belong to chemistry and not to the alchemy of the Wild*. An elemental speaking, that is, the earth speaking in the form of something like a sūtra, is the elemental force of the voiceless voice of the Buddha, what Dōgen (quoting SU Dongpo) in his 1240 fascicle "*Keisei Sanshoku* [*Valley Sounds, Mountain Colors*]" called the Great Earth's and the Buddha's "long broad tongue." The shaman heals with poetic alchemy.

II

Speaking of some of the remarkable ways that the patriarchs and other ancient Buddhas have transmitted the Dharma, Dōgen turned to the words of the great Song poet and lay Buddha Dharma practitioner, SU Dongpo (the pen name of the Song Dynasty poet and statesman SU Shi). Su was enlightened when he heard the sound of a mountain stream flowing in the night. In his poem "We Wash Our Bowls in This Water" from *Mountains and Rivers Without End*, Snyder quotes Dōgen's commentary on Su's remarkable words in the poem that Su had successfully presented to his teacher, Chan Master Zhaojiao Changzong of the Linji School, as proof of his awakening. Su, who "sat one whole night by a creek on the slopes of Mt. Lu," began: "The stream with its sounds is a long broad tongue / The looming mountain is a wide-awake body" (MR, 138). The voice of the water with its encompassing tongue alludes to one of the Buddha's canonical thirty-two characteristics. The river, covered in darkness, was the Buddha speaking. The imposing form—"looming"—of the mountain, that is, the mountain suggesting the looming of all form as such, is the manifesting body of the Buddha, whose ongoing wakefulness calls us to awaken. Mountains and rivers, form and emptiness, are the inseparable, impermanent earth song of the Buddha. The poem continues:

> Throughout the night, song after song (MR, 138)

Through the night, beyond visibility but through listening to the voice of the mountain-valley stream—Dōgen will later use language of seeing with one's ears and hearing with one's eyes—Su hears each and every thing ever taught in all possible schools of the Buddha Dharma, hearing not the mere words of the verses, but the great Buddha sea about which the verses were singing.[4] No time, no culture, no language, no gender, indeed, no particular species of life, (including humans) owns the Buddha Dharma. It is to hear the Great Earth in this present moment. And finally the poem concludes,

How can I speak at dawn? (MR, 138)

How does one transmit the Dharma? How does one speak the elemental language? How does one write a poem? Perhaps we could already suggest that this song is a deeply geological song, not in its current usage of the study of the history and laws of earth solids, for that is to confuse the earth with its looming forms, but in the archaic sense of the *logos* (λόγος) and song of *Gē* (Γῆ) fully *awakened* as *Gaia* (Γαῖα). We should clarify that we are not speaking merely of the earth that sustains us, but the *awakening* to the Great Earth, the earth as Tārā, who is not the mother of all beings but rather "the mother of Buddhas" and thereby the "mother of those beings who see through birth and death" (NH, 63). It is the awakening to the Great Earth and simultaneously (nondualistically) the Great Earth whispering (and sometimes screaming) to us a wakeup call. Snyder allows Dōgen to weigh in immediately:

Sounds of streams and shapes of mountains.
The sounds never stop and the shapes never cease.
Was it Su who woke
or was it the mountains and streams?
Billions of beings see the morning star
and all become Buddhas!
If *you*, who are valley streams and looming mountains,
can't throw some light on the nature of ridges and rivers,

who can? (MR, 138–139)

Awakening to Gaia, to the Great Earth as the Great Assembly of All Beings, is to awaken to each and every being, to the mattering of all beings. In seeking to unleash this elemental word, this word that we say not just from ourselves—it is not in the end just the human subject that is speaking—but from ourselves as "the mountains, rivers, and the great earth," we hear the long broad tongue of ourselves as bioregional song, as Snyder hears and dreams the Cascadian song in "Raven's Beak River At the End":

> Mind in the mountains, mind of tumbling water,
>   mind running rivers,
> Mind of sifting
>   flowers in the gravels
> At the end of the ice age
>   we are the bears, we are the ravens,
> We are the salmon
>   in the gravel
> At the end of the ice age (MR, 123)

In 1964, thirty-two years before finally finishing *Mountains and Rivers Without End*, but after eight years of already tinkering with it, Snyder told Gene Fowler that "More and more I am aware of very close correspondences between the external and the internal landscape. In my long poem, *Mountains and Rivers Without End*, I'm dealing with these correspondences, moving back and forth" (RW, 5). When Snyder and the Mahāyāna traditions more generally speak of Mind, they do not just speak of the mind that we habitually imagine to be inside of us (our internal landscape). It is also the Mind that is the Great Earth (the external landscape). "A billion worlds can be sat through within a single sitting" (S, 59), Dōgen tells us. To realize that the earth has the deep structure of your own mind is to realize that the mind has the same deep structure as the Great Earth. This realization is fully transitive and nondual. "Now, we are both in, and outside, the world at once. The only place this can be is the *Mind*. Ah, what a poem" (TI, 114)! In learning to breathe more elementally, that is, in Zazen and other meditative practices, I realize that my breath, my mind, is not just my breath or my mind.

> A soft breath, world-wide, of night and day,
>   rising, falling,
> The Great Mind passes by its own
> fine-honed thoughts,
>   going each way. (MR, 70–71)

Dōgen realized this and this is part of what makes his writing so resonant today. For example, in "*Keisei Sanshoku* [Valley Sounds, Mountain Colors]" we hear: "Saying that the self returns to the self is not contradicted by saying that the self is mountains, rivers, and the great earth" (S, 89).

In the fascicle "*Busshō* [Buddha Nature]," Dōgen claims to have inherited his discourse on the Great Earth from the Twelfth Ancestor, Aśvaghosha

(c. 80–c. 150 CE), who had maintained that "mountains, rivers, and the great earth are the ocean of Buddha nature" (S, 238). The most notable appearance of this articulation is the renowned kōan by the Tang Dynasty Linji School Chan Master, Qingyuan Weixin (Jp. Seigen Ishin). It can also be found in D. T. Suzuki's *Essays in Zen*, first series, which Snyder first read in 1951 when he was hitchhiking to Indiana to study anthropology and linguistics. "It catapulted me into an even larger space; and though I didn't know it at the moment, that was the end of my career as an anthropologist."[5] The poem was recorded in the thirteenth-century work, *Wudeng Huiyuan* (*Compendium of Five Lamps*):

> Thirty years ago, before I began the study of Zen, I said, "Mountains are mountains, waters are waters." After I got an insight into the truth of Zen through the instruction of a good master, I said, "Mountains are not mountains, waters are not waters." But after having attained the abode of final rest [that is, Awakening], I say, "Mountains are really mountains, waters are really waters."[6]

In the first stage of Zen practice, mountains and waters are just things among things. In the second stage, they are emptied of their self-being (*svabhāva*), that is, they are seen against the horizon of their lack of intrinsic, self-standing, independent, discrete being. In the final realization, mountains really are mountains and waters really are waters because they show themselves elementally in their dynamically evolving interdependence. Mountains and waters are the elements by which the images of mountains and rivers come and go in the temporality of their fragile impermanence. Mountains and rivers do not refer, as they do in Platonism, to a meaning remote to themselves. The Buddha nature or elemental Buddha sea of things is not a remote ontological reality underlying appearances. It is things in their suchness (*tathatā*), the way of things just as they elementally are. As Dōgen articulates it in "*Sokushin Zebutsu* [Mind Right Now is Buddha]," mind or consciousness (*shin*, 心) of mountains, rivers, and earth is not aware of something besides mountains, rivers, and earth:

> Thus, we know that the mind is mountains, rivers, and the earth; the mind is the sun, the moon, and the stars. What is said here is not more, not less. Mountains, rivers, and earth mind are just mountains, rivers, and the earth. There are no extra waves or sprays. The sun, the moon, and stars mind is just the sun, the moon, and the stars. There is no extra fog or mist. (S, 46)

Elemental earth mind, the mind of the mountains, rivers, and the Great Earth, does not add extra fog or mist to perception. (Platonism is a great and pervasive fog.) There is not some other thing that one perceives besides the things themselves. It is elemental perception, the elementality of perception as such.

How do mountains and rivers elementally comprise the Great Earth? Snyder deploys both the poetic word and prose. How do mountains and rivers speak with the long broad tongue in and between these various forms of writing? Traditionally, this relationship is the stormy and vexing antagonism between the philosophical essay and the work of art, but the theme that holds them together (the Great Earth and its practice of the Wild) invites us to think these two expressions *nondualistically*.

III

What is the relationship between art and nature? How are we to hear a line like the one that Snyder has the Mountain Spirit whisper: "All art and song / is sacred to the real. As such" (MR, 148)? Is this the word of the sūtra that articulates the holding together of song and thought, poetry and philosophy?

Speaking of his early Rinzai training, Snyder reflects that he

> came to see the yogic implications of "mountains" and "rivers" as the play between the tough spirit of willed self-discipline and the generous and loving spirit of concern for all living beings: a dyad presented in Buddhist iconography as the wisdom-sword-wielding Mañjuśrī, embodying transcendent insight, and his partner, Tārā, the embodiment of compassion, holding a lotus or a vase. I could imagine this dyad as paralleled in the dynamics of mountain uplift, subduction, erosion, and the planetary water cycle. (MR, 155)

Snyder characterized the poetic cycle of *Mountains and Rivers Without End* as "a sort of sūtra—an extended poetic, philosophic, and mythic narrative of the female Buddha Tārā" (MR, 158).[7] Wild language as elemental language and elemental language as the wild song of Tārā and Gaia is sūtra language. As we see more fully in the next chapter, sūtra language is not restricted to human language (at least in the European sense of humanism and the humanities). More elementally, it is geological language.

Snyder's decade of Zen training in Japan, including his work with Ruth Fuller Sasaki and his training under ODA Sessō Rōshi, was in Rinzai lineages. It was not, however, until he moved back to California that Snyder discovered the elemental language of the white heat of the beginning of what later came to be called the Sōtō School of Zen. "In the late seventies my thinking was invigorated by the translations from Dōgen's *Treasury of the True Law* [*Shōbōgenzō*] just then beginning to come out. His *Mountains and Waters Sūtra* is a pearl of a text" (MR, 157). These invigorating translations to which Snyder refers include Kazuaki TANAHASHI's watershed collection, *Moon in a Dewdrop*, which was published by North Point Press, at the time helmed by Snyder's publisher and friend, Jack Shoemaker (b. 1946). (He had cofounded the press with William Turnbull in 1979.) Snyder even released an audio recording of his readings of some of the fascicles from this collection (*The Teachings of Zen Master Dōgen*). But even before these translations appeared, Snyder recollects being the recipient of a smuggled translation of the *Sansui-kyō* from Carl Bielefeldt's MA thesis.[8]

Dōgen's *Sansui-kyō* (1240), *Mountains and Waters Sūtra*, brought many things together for Snyder. "Now it becomes possible for contemporary environmentalists, of wide and compassionate view, also to think of Dōgen a kind of ecologist. An *ecologist*, not just a Buddhist priest who had a deep sensibility for nature, but a protoecologist, a thinker who had remarkable insight deep into the way that wild nature works" (MHM, 161). Dōgen's title, *Sansui-kyō*, alludes to Chinese landscape painting, a powerful example of which opens *Mountains and Rivers Without End*. Snyder had already studied this tradition with the great Chiura OBATA (1885–1975) at Berkeley, becoming "aware of how the energies of mist, white water, rock formations, air swirls—a chaotic universe where everything is in place—are so much a part of the East Asian painter's world" (MR, 153). When Dōgen allows this paradoxically chaotic but not disorderly universe to speak (an early intuition of the crux of contemporary chaos theory), he resorts to phrases like "mountains, rivers, the great earth."

Dōgen's *Sansui-kyō* (山水經) is not itself a sūtra (*kyō*), nor is it a commentary on a canonical sūtra.[9] The sūtra is Tārā and Gaia themselves, which Dōgen, following a venerable Chinese tradition, calls *sansui* (Chinese *shan-shui*, 山水, mountains and waters). This is the term for something like "landscape," especially with reference to paintings, but it is not landscape in the typical sense of a panoptic view of scenery or a formal representation of what is "out there" to be seen. Rather it is the Great Earth as the interpenetration of yin and yang, waters and solids, emptiness and form, free, unconditioned ground and interdependent beings, in the spontaneous, organic autogenesis of Dao. *San* (山), mountain, rises into form in the most formidable of ways, as if it were an especially forceful and implacable expression of form's self-insistence, yet, it too flows, for *sui* (水), water, is pure elasticity, having no form of its own, yet capable of taking any form. *Sansui*, the insistence of form and its concomitant emptiness, and, transitively, emptiness in its dynamic shapeliness, is nature as both the stubborn, hard as a diamond, bright as the sun, aspiration of Fudō Myō-ō, the Immovable Wisdom King, and the dark as the moon, beneficently pliable, and softly overpowering compassion of Kannon, the bodhisattva Avalokiteśvara who looks down and hear the cries of the world.

In *Mountains and Rivers Without End*, in the first part of a section entitled "The Flowing," perhaps itself a way of thinking the manner in which mountains walk and flow as time, Snyder sings of the Blue-faced growling Fudō, / Lord of the Headwaters, making / Rocks of water, water out of rocks" (MR, 68). In the final poem of Snyder's earth sūtra, as he sings through the voice of Zeami's Nō play *Yamamba* (山姥, *Old Mountain Woman*),[10] we hear the words:

> Peaks like Buddhas   at the heights
>   send waters streaming down
> to the deep center of the turning world.
>
> And the Mountain Spirit always wandering
>   hillsides fade like walls of cloud
>   pebbles smoothed off sloshing in the sea
>
>   old woman mountain hears
> shifting sand
>   tell the wind
>   "nothingness is shapeliness"
>
> *Mountains will be Buddhas then* (MR, 145)

Mountains emerge as Buddhas when the shifting sands, pliable like water, shift and reform like Yamamba herself. In the *Sansui-kyō*, Dōgen meditates on the elemental words that Priest Daokai (1043–1118) of the Chinese Caodong (Sōtō) School offered to the assembly: "The green mountains are always walking; a stone woman gives birth to a child at night." The Green mountains walk, they flow not from the form of themselves, but discontinuously, as non-sequiturs, from the formless into form. This is the walking of mountains, a walking that derives not from what a mountain is formally, but from its seriatim shifting, its discontinuous manifestation, so to speak.

Walking manifests mountains and mountains, like all beings, express walking. The forms of being are not in time, deriving themselves from themselves. For something to be *in time*, it first has to be itself. But how is it possible for us to think of a mountain as something that began, endured through time, and then one day ended? To regard a mountain in this way, we have to think about it conceptually, to construe it with a concept as something fixed. When the mountain thereby becomes a fixed point of reference, time appears in the background (the *duration* of this abstraction that we construe as a selfsame mountain). If the mountain is not a fixed point of reference for time, however, time marks the emptiness of the form of the mountain (that a mountain is not first itself and then endures through time). Rather than a continuity through time, the mountain is time as discontinuity, as difference. Impermanence is not that a mountain does not endure forever, but rather that it does not endure at all because it is not first and foremost an identity to either endure or perish. Rather than thinking time from the perspective of the mountain, Dōgen thinks the mountain from the great imponderable sea of time.

Mountains express the emptiness of time itself—what Dōgen famously called *uji*, time-being—and hence one could also say that the stone woman, a barren mountain that produces no fruit from itself, gives birth "in the night," that is, from the watery, monstrous, elemental depths of time itself.[11] This is the Way of the Wild, the Way of the wondrous, even miraculous, Dharma (*myōhō*), each of its Dharma stages (*hōi*) unprethinkable.[12] If the mountain is no longer simply first and foremost a form, then the limits of expecting it to be more or less what it was before are exposed. What a mountain is *now* is not simply derived from what a mountain was *then*. It is a barren woman and it does not therefore give birth to itself, somehow perpetuating itself through time. A mountain in each and every moment expresses the Dharma—it is in each and every moment a dwelling stage of the Dharma—and hence calls for mindfulness, that is, cultivating an ongoing attentiveness to what it is now and here as an expression of the ongoing walking of the emptiness of time (giving birth in the night).

Hence, Dōgen can say that "a mountain always practices in every place" (S, 155) and "when your learning is immature, you are shocked by the words 'flowing mountains.' Without fully understanding even the words 'flowing water,' you drown in small views and narrow understanding" (S, 155–156).

Objects are not first discrete entities and then secondarily moving through time. Beings are empty and become anew, "like each time was the first" (MR, 130). This is the endless becoming of mountains and waters, being and time, that Dōgen called *kyōryaku*, what ABE Masao expansively translates as "passageless-passage." All of being is Buddha nature, but Buddha nature is the temporal conditions of time. This is the truth of the impermanence of Buddha nature: not that things are finite, but that they are ceaselessly emptied by time.[13] Because "being and time are identical in terms of the manifestation [*genzen*] of the Buddha nature" (SD, 88), mountains walk and the stone woman gives birth in the night.

Prior to this realization, we think that we are a fixed and permanent point that, as such, is the unswerving master perspective on all things. In "*Genjō Kōan* [Actualizing the Fundamental Point]," Dōgen likens this illusion to being on a boat and, because one cannot see the impermanence of one's own position, concluding that it is the land that is moving. This is the confused mind-set with which we initially perceive all beings (the ten thousand or myriad beings). In returning to the self in order to forget the self, one clarifies one's Original mind. "When you practice intimately and return to where you are, it will be clear that nothing at all has unchanging self" (S, 30). When the self falls away and is no longer the reference point for beings, the mountains and rivers without end confirm one. To forget the self is to be continuously actualized by all beings, all beings simultaneously casting away and experiencing the dropping away of the body and mind (Dōgen's famous *shinjin datsuraku*) (S, 30). This is the splendor of every moment, the depth of each day, each being, each moment, where all beings are inseparable from all beings. My Original Mind was not my personal private quotidian mind, but the "Great Mind" (MR, 73). My awakening and realization confirms the awakening and realization of all beings. The awakening and realization of all beings confirms my awakening and realization.

ABE Masao, too, is attuned to the manner in which Dōgen articulates this realization of the Great Earth's ongoing realization (in the double sense of ever realizing anew its endless becoming real anew) in terms of mountains and waters:

> This is, at the same time, the world of self-fulfilling *samādhi* [concentrated Zen awareness] and the world of the spontaneous manifestation of true suchness (*genjōkōan*). In this world, turning the mountains, rivers, and the Great Earth into the Self as well as turning

the Self into the mountains, rivers, and the Great Earth takes place.[14] It is also expressed as, "We cause the mountains, rivers, earth, sun, moon, and stars to practice and conversely the mountains, rivers, earth, sun, moon, and stars cause us to practice."[15] This is the world of the non-obstruction of things and things that "is turning both self and other." (SD, 97–98)

This was Dōgen's own practice of the Wild, what he called *bendōwa*, negotiating Dao and wholeheartedly practicing it.[16] In the fascicle of the same name we find the following astonishing claim: In Zen mind, one realizes that

> trees, grasses, and land involved in this all emit a bright and shining light, preaching the profound and incomprehensible Dharma; and it is endless. Trees and grasses, wall and fence expound and exalt the Dharma for the sake of ordinary people, sages, and all living beings. Ordinary people, sages, and all living beings in turn preach and exalt the Dharma for the sake of trees, grasses, wall and fence. (HDS, 13)[17]

Hee-Jin Kim rightly insists that the *sansui* or mountains and waters practice of Dōgen, which included his peregrinations through the mountains of China looking for a teacher as well as the remote mountain location of his temple, Eihei-ji, was not the "romantic exaltation of them which we see, for example, in nature mysticism, any more than it is the scientific and technical manipulation and exploitation of nature." The "naïve veneration or exaltation of nature," evident in the more reactionary, infantile, antiscientific giddiness about trees and birds in the worst excesses of Romanticism, was for Dōgen "a defiled view of nature, enslaving humans in a new captivity."[18] Rather Kim sees in Dōgen's "love" of nature "not a deification of nature, but the radicalization of nature—nature in its selflessness. Only then is nature undefiled and natural" (DKM, 191).

Dōgen is not advocating, nor would he likely recognize as sensible, any call to return to a pristine, undefiled nature. There is "no 'original condition' which once altered will never be redeemed" (PS, 240). Dōgen was not an advocate of wilderness in the sense of places unperturbed by human habitation. There is no unmediated access to nature, no thing in itself in some private reality beyond our ensconcement in the veil of *māyā* and its web of representations or delusions. Nowhere in Dōgen or Snyder is there any kind of New Age fantasy of a lost and intrinsically beneficent and harmonious Eden.

Awakening for Dōgen is always to be awake to conditions and causes, to be free for the paradoxical play of karma (the free play of what must be). The infinite ground of the Wild is not a thing, either in itself or as a series of representations originating in human subjectivity. Being mindful of things "just as they are" does not mean that one develops a special kind of seeing that can penetrate the illusions that bind others. It is, rather, a different kind of seeing and a different relationship in consciousness to the causes and conditions of karma. One does not break through to reality beyond a veil of illusion but rather overcomes one's own ignorance (*avidyā*, literally, not seeing) regarding the interdependent play of causes and conditions.

We should also be careful not to rush to the other extreme: If there no pristine *Ding an sich* called nature, then it must all be a representation seated in human subjectivity and its interests. Yes, the Wild is *always* interpreted, and human beings engage it within the historical milieu that grants them access to it. This is not, however, to advocate the subsumption of the Wild under culture and obscure its inassimilable alterity. The living core of the Wild is not an object that resists the advances of a discerning subject nor is it the product of the subject's own mind (as it is in Idealism). We are not separate from the Wild, studying it as something beside ourselves. We are always *of* it and hence the question is not whether we have a relationship to the Wild, but rather *what kind of relationship is it*. Whether it is a dominating relationship or a more mindful relationship, we are involved in a set of relations whose depths we cannot plumb. The infinite depth of our immanence is the alterity of the home within which we emerge. And so Snyder rightly laments in "Is Nature Real?":

> It's a real pity that many in the humanities and social sciences are finding it so difficult to handle the rise of "nature" as an intellectually serious territory. For all of the talk of "the other" in everybody's theory these days, when confronted with a genuine Other, the nonhuman realm, the response of the come-lately anti-nature intellectuals is to circle the wagons and declare that nature is really part of culture. (GSR, 388–389)

That nature would be an extension of culture is the global symptom of what Heidegger called the *Gestell* and, as Heidegger warned, when this subsumption is complete, Dasein can never, as it did so dramatically in *Being and Time*, following Augustine, come to experience itself as a question, as a source of distress and turmoil. This danger allows us to hear Dōgen's celebrated counsel in a new resonance: The Buddha Way is to study the self, but to study the self is to forget the self and to awaken to all of the Wild (*Genjō Kōan*, S, 30). Wandering, Snyder somewhat erotically sings his earth song:

The root of me
hardens and lifts to you,
thick flowing river,

my skin shivers. I quit

making this poem. (MR, 72)

In a sense, the river composes these words as I quit imagining that it is I who can take full responsibility for "my" poems. Even the erotic tinge of this poem speaks less to the sport of sexual conquest and more to the creative play of form and emptiness. It is closer to the "cross-legg'd" play of *yab-yum* ("father-mother," i.e., the creative union of wisdom and compassion, form and emptiness): "always new, same stuff . . like each time was the first" (MR, 130). Entering the backcountry of the Wild requires neither discerning the Wild as a pristine object nor dismissing it as a mere subjective representation. To study the Buddha Way is to study the Self but to study the Self is to forget the Self. To forget the Self is to awaken to the backcountry:

We were following a long river into the mountains.
Finally we rounded a ridge and could see deeper in—
the farther peaks stony and barren, a few alpine trees.
Ko-san and I stood on a point by a cliff, over a
rock-walled canyon. Ko said, "Now we have come to
where we die." I asked him—what's up there,
then—meaning the further mountains.
"That's the world after death." I thought it looked
just like the land we'd been traveling, and couldn't
see why we should have to die.
Ko grabbed me and pulled me over the cliff—
both of us falling. I hit and I was dead. I saw
my body for a while, then it was gone.
Ko was there too. We were at the bottom of the gorge.
We started drifting up the canyon. "This is the
Way to the back country." (MR, 55–56)

Kō-san, a Zen teacher, has helped peck at the egg shell that Snyder is trying to crack from within; as he liberates himself from himself, he undergoes what Zen famously calls the Great Death (*daishi*). Kō-san alludes to Sōkō MORINAGA with whom Snyder practiced at Daitoku-ji.[19] As Katsunori YAMAZATO, who translated *Mountains and Rivers Without End* into Japanese, aptly articulates it: "To awaken to a new dimension of consciousness, one has to transcend the mundane world, and only after the destruction of the mundane ego is one capable of finding 'the way to the back country.'"[20] In the backcountry of awakening language, we find ourselves with the mountains that Dōgen insisted were fond of wise people and sages.

> They are what we are, we are what they are. . . . No hierarchy, no equality. No occult and exoteric, no gifted kids and slow achievers. No wild and tame, no bound and free, no natural and artificial. Each totality its own frail self. . . . This, thusness, is the nature of the nature of nature. The wild in wild. So the blue mountains walk back to the shop, to the desk, to the stove. We sit on the park bench and let the wind and rain drench us. The blue mountains walk out and put another coin in the parking meter, and go down to the 7–11. (PW, 110–111)

In the final chapter of *The Practice of the Wild* called "Grace," Snyder explains that at his house they say a Buddhist grace, which begins, "We venerate the Three Treasures [teachers, the wild, and friends]" (PW, 185). The three treasures are universally acknowledged by all negotiators of the Buddha Dharma to be the Buddha, which Snyder, using his own *upāya* or skillful means, renders as "teachers," the Saṅgha, the community of practitioners, whom Snyder renders as "friends," and finally, and most strikingly, the Dharma, which Snyder renders as "the Wild."

In what manner can the Dharma, the very matter that is transmitted from Buddha Dharma to Buddhist negotiator, be translated as the Wild?

It depends on our capacity to hearken to what is silenced in the word "wild" in common parlance. In the latter "wild" and "feral [*ferus*]" are "largely defined in our dictionaries by what—from a human standpoint—it is not. It cannot be seen by this approach for what it is" (PW, 9). Hence, a wild animal is an animal that has not been trained to live in our house (undomesticated) and has not been successfully subjected to our rule (unruly). When we tire of the mores to which we regulate our behaviors, we imagine that "we go wild," as if this were the way of all nonhuman forms of life. To call someone an "animal" is to associate them with the outlaws and the uncivilized. If something is not subject to the rules of our culture, then it is the nomadic wildness that terrified Kant as wanton savagery, as "independence from laws."[21]

But what happens if we "turn it the other way"? What is the wild *to the Wild*? Animals become "free agents, each with its own endowments, living within natural systems" (PW, 9). As Snyder begins to explore this turn, he indicates the ways in which the Wild "comes very close to being how the Chinese define the term *Dao*, the *way* of Great Nature: eluding analysis, beyond categories, self-organizing, self-informing, playful, surprising, impermanent, insubstantial, independent, complete, orderly, unmediated . . ." (PW, 10). And the Dao, as we know from the rich interpenetration of Mahāyāna and Daoist traditions in East Asia, is "not far from the Buddhist term Dharma with its original senses of forming and firming" (PW, 10). The early Daoists spoke of Dao as "the great mother." The Wild is the "back country," but that country is not only in the mountains or, as we see in chapter 4, "where the bears are" (PW, 30). It is also found in the depths of our own minds, at the heart of language, repressed even within the heart of our metropolises.

We are not in an exclusive disjunction of being either wild *or* civilized. We *are* the Wild. "'Mountains and waters' is a way to refer to the totality of the process of nature. As such it goes beyond the dichotomies of purity and pollution, natural and artificial. The whole with its rivers and valleys, obviously includes farms, fields, villages, cities, and the (once comparatively small) dusty world of human affairs" (PW, 109). We are not civilized animals who every now and again escape the drudgeries of our autonormalized modes of being by going wild and becoming party animals. "Wildness is not just the 'preservation' of the world, it *is* the world" (PW, 6). The Wild is the self-organizing autoproductivity of our being and being as such. "'Wild' as process is universal" (BF, 130); it is a "name for the process of the impermanence and constant flow of change of phenomena, as constantly going without human intervention" (NH, 84).

Although I do not think that this has been sufficiently appreciated by those who oppose Snyder's embrace of the Wild, he is clearly not embracing the legal definition of the Wild as "a place without noticeable human impact or permanent presence" (BF, 129)—almost as if we were desperately trying to spare some places from the pernicious modes of human habitation that have gone into overdrive since the industrial revolution and the ascent of capitalism. The Wild is not something outside of or beyond or wholly otherwise than us. That we think so is part of the nub of the ecological crisis. The landscape within is the landscape without and vice versa. The Wild is within (language as well as the depth of the mind's pure luminosity) and without (the Great Earth) but in all of its strata it comprises us.

Snyder is not lamenting the existence of cities, although he does lament that we have largely lost the sensibility that urban life has its own practice of the Wild. (He considered San Francisco an exception, at least before its current occupation by the masters of capital; what Snyder laments about American cities is not that they are cities, but rather that they are such inhospitable and alienating cities.)

In *Mountains and Rivers Without End*, Snyder takes an owl's eye perspective on Los Angeles ("Night Song of the Los Angeles Basin"), seeing its "calligraphy of cars" (MR, 64). The calligraphic stroke attempts to take the form or mountain (*yang*) element and make it dance and come alive, rife with energy, by playing itself off against the emptiness or *yin* element of the white paper. The character is animated as much by its background emptiness as its foregrounded form. Nothingness comes to animate the character just as the owl can see the repressed life and wildness seeping through the suffocating Los Angeles basin. Yes, the "owl calls," but it is a "late-rising moon" (MR, 66), that is, a slow awakening. But if the moon rises in Los Angeles, it is because, as the owl teaches us, it rises everywhere. To receive this teaching, however, we need in some manner or another to open our true Dharma eye. The owl does not discriminate between the Wild and the civilized (although some no doubt prefer more amenable habitats than our cities). Snyder later applies his Dharma eye to New York City ("Walking the New York Bedrock Alive in the Sea of Information"), "wide and waving in the Sea of Economy" (MR, 99).

The nonduality of the true Dharma owl does not maintain an absolute distinction between national parks and contemporary megacities. When asked in 1973 if he would write differently if he lived in a city rather than Kitkitdizze, Snyder responded, "probably not too differently, especially as I'm learning to see cities as natural objects" (RW, 37). Cities, too, are wild processes. They do have one disadvantage, however: although the owl can see the Wild in Los Angeles, Angelinos have a hard time learning that the etiquette of the Wild asks them to aspire to the eye of the owl.

IV

Snyder is not just asking us to come to a new theoretical realization. He is attempting to awaken another mode of consciousness. Understanding the Wild is not the same thing as caring about the Wild, although if you care about the Wild, this will likely motivate you to better understand both its global and local aspects. Conducting debates about public policy are necessary, but they are not sufficient to move beyond our corporate-capitalist-grab-and-run posture. We also have to open our true Dharma eyes.

> To transform public policy in regard to the oceans and air, forests, and population questions, and to move toward saving endangered species, both require reaching the very hearts of whole societies.
>
> This is not a work of the scientists. Their research is essential to us, but to change the way contemporary human beings live on earth is a kind dharma work, a work for dedicated followers of the Way who because of their practice and insight can hope to balance wisdom and compassion and help open the eyes of others. I think that Buddhism, and especially old Shamon Dōgen, has something to show us in the matter of how to go about this. (MHM, 163)

Ecological policies would also be a question of practice, not just the rational and bureaucratic execution of tasks. This points to a dimension of action that Dōgen called *shingi*, pure standards or rules, originally referring to the protocols for monastic life at Eihei-ji. Even in the *Shōbōgenzō*, the Dōgen who could write breathlessly about the inseparability of being and time (*uji*) was the same Dōgen who could in the next moment write about the proper manner of cleaning your body (*Senjō*), including how to wipe your ass after defecating in the woods after practicing Zazen outdoors,[22] or washing your face (*Semmen*).[23] "It is not only cleansing the body and mind, but also cleansing the entire land" (S, 49). The loss of the practice of countering bad breath by rinsing the mouth, scraping the tongue, and then chewing on a little *yōji* or willow twig, indicates that the "decline of the great way of buddha ancestors is beyond measure" (S, 67). Moreover, "without washing the face, all the practices would lack authenticity" (S, 70). Sewing and caring for your robe (the *kāṣāya* or *kesa*) is very important because "there is more merit in seeing the Buddha robe, hearing the teaching of it, and making offerings to it than in presiding over the billion worlds" (S, 113). When sewing it, however, one optimally takes patches from whatever discarded cloth one can find, including "burned cloth, cloth chewed by oxen, cloth chewed by rats, and cloth from corpses," even "excrement-cleaning cloth" (S, 119).

Monastic practice (or just engaging in some Zen practice as part of one's daily life) in its deepest and most clarified manifestation is not in the end a retreat from the world, but an effort to more fully realize the Great Earth that one already *is*. In this spirit of *shingi*, Snyder suggests that Dōgen's "*Instructional Text for Forest Management, Ocean and Wetland Restoration, and Third World Crisis Intervention* would be that guide for dharma activists and administrators—the 'Tenzo-kyōkun,' 'Instructions to the Head Cook'" (MHM, 165).

Of all of Dōgen's *shingi* fascicles, the *Tenzo-kyōkun* continues to have the greatest impact. Given the rigors of food preparation, the head cook (*tenzo*) for the monastery (or even growing vegetables and cooking as part of one's daily practice) has far less opportunity to practice Zazen and do all the other sorts of things that one associates with traditional practice. Our prejudices tempt us to assume that the *tenzo* gets the short end of the deal, preparing food so that others can practice Zazen. That assumes that there is something lowly about food preparation and other "real work" like washing your face, wiping your ass, cleaning the dishes, sweeping the floor, scrubbing the toilet, and changing the oil in your car. Zazen is not a flight from the mundane, but rather the realization of the everyday profundity of real work.

Growing and eating food is not just fuel in order to have the energy to do more important things. As we see in chapter 5, it is to participate in the *puja* and potlatch that is the great exchange of energies that comprises the passageless passage of the Great Earth. Without wholesome food there is no Zazen. Looking at the nightmare of fast food, industrial farming, rampant addiction, the voracious overconsumption of animal products, especially their flesh, and the use of fossil fuels to ensure that we can eat whatever we want whenever we want,[24] regardless of season and location, it is easy to see that we are as mindful of food (and our own bodies) as we are of our place and our Earth. Such mindlessness—the spiritual connection between fast food, ecological pollution, and the Sixth Great Extinction event—is at the heart of the current ecological crisis. If you cannot take the time to clean your own dishes and to learn to relish doing so, the forests, oceans, wetlands, as well as our human sisters and brothers in the Global South as well as those marginalized everywhere by our hatred or indifference, will continue to languish.

Dōgen instructed the *tenzo* not to lose either "the eye of oneness [the true Dharma eye] or the eye that discerns differences [the capacity to be mindful of the specifics of food and the detailed practice of its preparation]."[25] At the end of Dōgen's fascicle, we find the phrase, "Written in the spring of 1237 to instruct later wise people who study Dao" (DPS, 49). The *tenzo* cultivates mindfulness in response to our mindlessness around food (itself a symptom of a more generalized mindlessness). One practices attuning oneself to the Dao in food preparation.[26] "If you do not have the mind of the Way, then all of this hard work is meaningless and not beneficial" (DPS, 33). We should not underestimate the *tenzo*: She is working to save all sentient beings beginning with our somnolence around food. Dōgen cites an ancient master: "When steaming rice, regard the pot as your own head; when washing rice, know that the water is your own life" (DPS, 33). The *tenzo* prepares food *nyohō*, in accordance with Dharma (DPS, 39) and this is also how we should approach our wetlands, rather than leaving them to the ravages of build-and-run developers.

2

Geology
(Poetic Word)

The Mountain Spirit whispers back:
"All art and song
is sacred to the real.
As such." (MR, 148)[1]

I

How does the long broad tongue sing (MR, 140)? How does language arise "unbidden" (PW, 18)? Why does Snyder think that the poetic word is indispensible to an engagement with the ecological crisis?

Snyder told Peter Barry Chowka that "practice is to life as poetry is to spoken language. So as poetry is the practice of language, 'practice' is the practice of life. At any time when the attention is there fully, then all of the Bodhisattva's acts are being done" (RW, 134). As we saw at the end of the last chapter: washing the dishes, teaching classes, pulling weeds, chopping wood, writing poetry, and defending biodiversity: with the true Dharma eye, all are "real work."

Yet, no matter how well the real work has been done—no matter how extraordinary the poem, how well cut the wood, how penetrating the philosophical analysis, how clean the house—it has not been completed for all time, for all beings in all places. The real work is like "Marpa purifying Milarepa" (MR, 110). Under his teacher's instruction, the great Tibetan master and poet Milarepa "four times built a tower of stone / like each time was the first" (MR, 130). As soon as he finished building the stone tower, Marpa instructed Milarepa to take it apart and build it again. (Snyder remembers that during his Zen training in Kyoto, his fellow monks resisted his practical suggestions, claiming that the point of *samu* or work was to do the work, not achieve a goal beyond the work.) I remember my own instruction in the Zen monastery: even if the floor is completely clean, find a way to make it cleaner! The real work is practice and practice is an end in itself, not a means to a goal, what Dōgen called the oneness of practice and realization (*shushō-ittō*). The end is found always in the practice, not at the end of the practice or otherwise beyond the practice. We build the stone tower of the poem or the philosophical reflection again and again. That is not a Sisyphusian curse. It is the practice of the Wild, the dance in which mountains and rivers confirm us and we confirm mountains and rivers.

Each time we build a little house, no matter how well we do it, of course, it is fragile and impermanent. In "Old Woodrat's Stinky House," we hear that "A spoken language works / for about five centuries / lifespan of a douglas fir" (MR, 121). For all their majesty and despite their global ambitions, languages come and go, and they pale in comparison to stately elders like the bristlecone pines, living in arid and harsh conditions, but thriving because, like the Buddha, they know how much is enough and how to be present to their place. Snyder's poetry and essays, as well as this book, are impermanent and fragile. What human words capture the long and quietly spoken eloquence of the bristlecone? And what is a bristlecone to the walking mountains of geological processes? "Ice ages come one hundred and fifty million years apart / last about ten million / then warmer days return" (MR, 121). And all of this pales before the age and magnitude of the cosmos. . . .

Such thoughts humble the language in which they are articulated, bringing it to its edge. Nonetheless, language is not just a modest event within the cosmos. It can, without abdicating its modesty and finitude, also seek to express the whole universe. Dōgen, for example, esteemed the phrase, *All the universe [the entire world of the ten directions] is one bright pearl*, itself the teaching of the late Tang Dynasty Chan Master XUANSHA Shibei (835–908; Jp. Gensha Shibi). Dōgen turned to this expression in an early fascicle from the *Shōbōgenzō* called "*Ikka Myōju* [One Bright Pearl]."[2]

For Dōgen, this expression did not *mean* anything if by that we mean Frege's sense (communication of an idea) or reference (that to which an idea refers). It was not a discursively warranted claim about the nature of anything in particular. It did not proffer a philosophical account. It was not a proposition or a premise. Dōgen had no patience with those who pursued propositional discourse about the Dharma, and warned his monks to be wary of the "briars and brambles of word-attachment" (HDS, 2), and not to "get caught up in skillfully turned words and phrases" (HDS, 17) and not be "enmeshed in the traps and snares of words and letters" (HDS, 18). Dharma transmission is not accomplished through the exchange of information about the Dharma. Rather, when the young Xuansha, who had been a fisherman, floated down the Nantai River, like many other fishermen, "he did not even expect the Golden Fish that comes to you unbidden without angling for it" (HDS, 32). He did not expect the communicative expressivity of sudden—unbidden—awakening. Having been surprised by the appearance of this fish, Xuansha aspired to depart from the dusty world and practice the Way wholeheartedly.

How then is Dharma expressed and thereby communicated when *expression* is not *sensu stricto* fundamentally meaningful and *communication* is not the successful exchange of ideas? It is not a question of holding or promoting the superior doctrine, for with authentic practice, humans "have flowed into the Way [*Dao*] drawn by grasses and flowers, mountains and running water. They have received the lasting impression of the Buddha-seal by holding soil, rocks, sand, and pebbles." Indeed, a "single mote of dust suffices to turn the great Dharma wheel" (HDS, 17). "*One bright pearl* is able to express reality without naming it, and we can recognize this pearl as its name. One bright pearl communicates directly through all time" (HDS, 34).

The poetic word is *expressive*. As such, it is not necessarily a word *about* something, but rather *is* in some manner the Wild in its manifold and dynamically evolving processes. It both awakens the audience to the Wild and reveals that the Wild, beyond all concepts and experiences, is always at play. "The true poem is walking that edge between what can be said and that which cannot be said. That is the real razor's edge" (RW, 21). Like Bashō's haiku, "the words stop but the meaning goes on" (RW, 22). It does not so much name the Wild as *express* it, and, in so doing, awaken one compassionately to it. Snyder strives to say the *one bright pearl* in his own way for our own time of human folly in relationship to the Great Earth.

Snyder has often spoken of such "all-embracing" language and its capacity to awaken. Reminiscing about his early relationship to Daisetz Suzuki, Snyder recalled that "for us, in our energy of the fifties, early Buddhism, Laozi, Gandhi, Thoreau, Kropotkin, and Zen were all one teaching. We stood for original human nature and spontaneous creative spirit."[3] This "one teaching" and its auditors were not separate, even at the beginning, from the places they inhabited. "We were people of the Far West, loving our continent for its great wild beauty, feeling no ties to Europe. Our politics and aesthetics were one. Dr. Suzuki's exposition of Zen gave us an idea of a religion and an all-embracing view of nature to augment that of scientific Ecology, which had already begun to instruct us."[4] Zen practice, science, art, and mindful inhabitation were inseparable.

In this respect, one should not, however, automatically count Snyder as part of the intellectual trend that espouses that everything is a text. Nature, in the sense of the Wild, is definitely not a book that can be theologically and philosophically deciphered as it was in the European Middle Ages.[5] That disposition has been generally discredited by both philosophy and science. A far subtler and posttheological variant on that position has emerged, this time charging that the "Wild" is simply a "social construction." Snyder is always careful not to deny the role of human projection in perception—the problem of what both Mahāyāna and Advaita Vedanta have called *māyā*. But he denies that this means that the Great Earth is just one big social construct, that the Wild can be subsumed into culture, and that practice is hopelessly in thrall to ideology. Moreover, the overreach of the "social construction" position that absorbs the earth into culture inadvertently plays into the hands of the earth exploiters. "The attacks on nature and wilderness from the ivory towers come at just the right time to bolster global developers, the resurgent timber companies . . . and those who trash the Endangered Species Act" (GSR, 388).

Biodiversity in itself, not ideology about biodiversity, "is essential to planetary health for all" and should be protected (GSR, 388).[6] As we see in our concluding chapter, earth democracy or Earth Saṅgha, is of paramount importance and at the heart of awakening and ecological conversion. When the Wild is merely a text,[7] regardless of all its alterity, undecidability, and slippage, it is reduced to a domain that can only understood and valued in relation to us, even as it contests us. The Wild is not subsumed to our processes but rather our processes belong to its processes. We need more radical practices of getting over ourselves, a new variant of what Robinson Jeffers dubbed the "inhuman." "*Wild* is the process that surrounds us all, self-organizing nature" (GSR, 389) and human language and culture are a part of those processes, albeit currently ones in runaway.

Snyder is no reactionary and this is not to dismiss the importance of deconstructive thought. "Deconstruction, done with a compassionate heart and the intention of gaining wisdom, becomes the Mahāyāna Buddhist logical and philosophical exercise that plumbs to the bottom of deconstruction and comes back with compassion for all beings. Deconstruction without compassion is self-aggrandizement" (GSR, 387–388).

Snyder carefully avoids the potentially self-aggrandizing relegation of everything to a text, which risks making the Wild a subset of human processes. Rather he thinks of the Great Earth, including human processes (language, culture, science, art, etc.), as a *sūtra*. Not everything is a text, but all of being is Buddha nature, that is to say, a sūtra. Snyder has explicitly come to consider *Mountains and Rivers Without End* itself "as a sort of sūtra" (MR, 160): a little book that, like Wovoka's hat or Baby Krishna's mouth, contains all of the spirits of all places on the Great Earth, past, present, and future. To read a sūtra is not to read a text that subsumes the Wild into the politics and intellectual investments of a particular culture. A sūtra through and through resists the absorption of the Great Earth into a globalized world and its concomitant "reading" practices. The Earth itself, as we are also finding out the hard way, also resists this. In a way, this is because the Great Earth itself is a sūtra and to read it is to die to oneself and enter the "back country," living and thinking in its wild processes. It is to break through "global consciousness" [centralized technocracy] to "planetary mind . . . which recognizes the possibility of one earth with all of its diversity" (RW, 126).

II

Mountains and Rivers Without End begins with Snyder contemplating a remarkable horizontal hand scroll called *Ch'i Shan Wu Chin* (*Endless Streams and Mountains*)[8] by an unknown artist from the Northern Song Dynasty. In 1953 it made its way to Turtle Island and, purchased through the Hanna Fund, it now resides in the Cleveland Museum of Art,[9] "which sits on a rise that looks out toward the waters of Lake Erie" (MR, 8). (The Hanna Fund was bequeathed by Leonard C. Hanna Jr. who made his fortune as a partner in M. A. Hanna Co., a major Cleveland iron-ore house.) It can be heartbreaking to reflect that "Ohio" was the Shawnee word for "beautiful" (RW, 59). In a city that conspicuously bears the wounds and scars of its history of coal, iron, and steel production, overlooking a lake (and its trade routes) that were inseparable from this industrial explosion, sits this scroll by an unknown artist or artists, comprised of at least five styles of *shan-shui* painting, perhaps expressing an historical progression of *shan-shui* styles, perhaps expressing the five houses or schools of Zen, but in any case, certain sections "emphasize the human in the midst of nature, while other scenes, reminiscent of other styles, depict an elemental landscape of hard-edged rock and water."[10]

In Snyder's accounting of things, *shan-shui* painting scrolls, unlike *shan-shui* poetry, arrive relatively late on the scene. "Paintings of large vistas did not appear until around the tenth century. This was after two-and-a-half millennia of self-aware civilization in the basins of the Ho and Chiang. They are at their most vigorous from mid-Song through the Yuan and early Ming—exactly when much of China was becoming deforested" (MR, 159). More microscopic subjects like birds, insects, bamboo leaves, and fruits eventually replaced the looming mountains and rivers, perhaps suggesting the further eclipse of our presence to the Wild. In *The Practice of the Wild*, Snyder tells us that "nature description is a kind of writing that comes with civilization and its habits of collection and classification" and hence landscape poetry does not begin in earnest until the fifth century, despite there having been fifteen hundred years of Chinese song and poetry—the Chinese had to become "removed enough from their own mountains and rivers to aestheticize them" (PW, 23).

The ascendancy of *shan-shui* painting from the mid-Sung through the Yüan and early Ming dynasties (and its enduring popularity to this day) did not merely attest to mountains as a symbol of the vanishing Wild as if any nonflat geological formations could be regarded as mountains. When Dōgen claims that "mountains are apart from the human world" and that it is a "fact" that they are "fond of wise people and sages" (*Sansui-kyō*, S, 163), he is also likely aware that mountains were what we now call the "back country." They literally mark the edge of civilization and agriculture—they were too steep, remote, and inaccessible even for terraced rice fields. This made the mountains a suitable refuge for Buddhists, outlaws, and any other outliers from civilized life and hence Dōgen tells us that the "imperial power has no authority over the wise people in the mountains" (S, 163).

In his most recent work (named after the Daoist Zhuangzi's name for the Great Earth), *The Great Clod: Notes and Memoirs on Nature and History in East Asia*, Snyder observes that already in the Tang Dynasty, despite its extraordinarily cosmopolitan culture, "wild habitats" were slowly but surely "shrinking before a relentlessly expanding agricultural society" (GC, 64). Snyder likened this gradual but implacable erosion to a frog being slowly boiled alive in water.

> The history of environment in China can be understood in terms of the frog in hot water. A frog tossed into a pan of boiling water, it is said, will jump right out. A frog placed in a pan of cold water over a slow flame will not leap out, and soon it's too late. (GC, 64)

Despite the triumphalism of the supposed "progress" brought forward by the industrial revolution and the rise of capitalism, human cultures all over the earth are frogs belatedly discovering that the water is starting to boil.

The Orientalist gaze turned longingly toward an imaginary China that was supposedly more in tune with the Wild. It is simply false, however, to suppose that all Buddhist cultures are ipso facto more ecologically enlightened than non-Buddhist cultures. For example, Mark Elvin's sobering and profound study of the three millennia of mounting ecological catastrophe in China, *The Retreat of the Elephants: An Environmental History of China*, dispels the fantasy that the Daoist and Chan traditions that began in Classical China, which rightly remain inspiring for contemporary ecological practice, did very much to stem the ecological degradation in anthropogenic China. "Four thousand years ago there were elephants in the area that was later to become Beijing . . . and in most of the rest of what was later to be China. Today, the only wild elephants in the People's Republic are those in a few protected enclaves in the Southwest, up against the border with Burma."[11]

In both Daoism and Chan Buddha Dharma, the Saṅgha includes all sentient beings, but this did not prevent the decimation of Chinese elephant populations. "There seems to be no case for thinking that, some details apart, the Chinese anthropogenic environment was developed and maintained in the way it was over the long run for more than three millennia because of particularly characteristic Chinese beliefs or perceptions. Or, at least, not in comparison with the massive effects of the pursuit of power and profit" (RE, 471). How efficacious can the Chan elements of a culture hope to be against the greed of empire? As efficacious as possible, no doubt, but this also teaches us that we must nonetheless take responsibility for a world that exceeds our capacity for saving it. The grounds of Chan temples at least "became the last refuges of huge old trees; in fact the present-day reconstruction of original forest cover in north China is done to a great extent by plotting the distribution of relict stands on temple grounds" (GC, 64).

The slowly heating water was already underway long before either the Tang Dynasty or the ascendancy of *shan-shui* scroll paintings in the mid-Song. Following Burton Watson and others, Snyder regards XIE Lingyun (385–433)[12] as the transition point from the "Wild" experience of the earth as inseparable from the human habitat in "fields and gardens poetry [園詩, *tianyuan shi*]" to *shan-shui shi* or mountains and waters poetry (山水詩). "By the Six Dynasties, the view moved back and became more panoramic."[13] Despite the political machinations that led to his execution by beheading,

Xie, who extensively explored the mountains, "opened up the landscape—'mountains and waters'—to the poetic consciousness for all time" (GSR, 289). These poems, despite the retreat of the earth and the poetic word's striving to reawaken its force in language, were not nostalgic, despite the travails of "civilized" life and its toll on human consciousness:

> They are not really about landscapes or scenery. . . . Mountains and rivers were seen to be the visible expression of cosmic principles; the cosmic principles go back into silence, non-being, emptiness; a Nothing that can produce the ten thousand things, and the ten thousand things will have that marvelous emptiness still at the center. So the poems are also "silent." (GSR, 293)

Perhaps one could make Snyder's point like this: When the bioregion is not jeopardized by the manner in which we are part of it, we *are* our bioregion; we *are* the self-developing, self-creating movement of mountains and waters that gives us the very possibility—as well as reverence-worthy gift—of our being and life ways. This, perhaps, is the elemental age of gardens and fields. When the bioregion comes under extreme threat, and, in a very real sense, our destructive behaviors are also self-destructive, both to us as a species and to our species being in its interdependence with the complex dynamic of its bioregional home, then mountains and rivers emerge in art and religious practice as something not only desecrated and taken for granted, but something whose fading value needs to be resuscitated. In a sense, the practice of the Wild becomes the practices in which we cultivate mindfulness for the endangered bioregion that we are as well as the grievous harm that we exact upon the life forms whose space we share. *As our way of being holds our elemental being in abeyance, our practice must become increasingly elemental.*

This is a key element to Snyder's own Zen practice at the Ring of Bone Zendo, which he helped build in 1982 and which was named after a phrase in a poem by his friend and former Reed classmate Lew Welch who disappeared in 1971 after leaving a suicide note.[14] Unfortunately, but perhaps unavoidably, some of the early Turtle Island appropriations of Japanese Zen erred on the side of assimilating Zen too quickly and cavalierly into the prevailing aspects of American culture, including some of its countercultural expressions. If one errs too much on the side of assimilation, Zen loses its power to contest our habits of being.

The antidote, however, is not to turn the Zendo into a Japanese time capsule and export Japanese practices without any modification and skillful means. This would make Zen practice akin to the hastily exported new cults in Rome, which Snyder considered merely "symptomatic of the breakdown of the fabric of society" (NH, 30). The Ring of Bone Zendo is simultaneously "more orthodox, more Asian" than typical Zen Centers and their place within the mass market "smorgasbord of therapies" (NH, 30). At the same time, it is more local, more present to its particular place and time on Turtle Island, including to the stories and myths that belong to its indigenous peoples. This also meant for Snyder resisting the Japanese professionalization of Zen. Although the latter retains an extraordinary rigor, it often does so at the expense of spontaneity and surprise. Hence the Ring of Bone Zendo "was not so much Zen as it was Chan. By that I mean not so narrowly monastic and Japanese, but more 'Chinese'—earlier, less codified, more ecumenical, ecological, playful."[15]

That being said, we paint and poeticize and sing and sit and otherwise practice ourselves as mountains and rivers precisely because it is no longer obvious that or how we are mountains and rivers. When we are painting more isolated and discrete forms of life—persimmons, dragonflies, itinerant Zen monks—the elemental has been all the more eclipsed. This is the time in which we fight to save the whales as an isolated species without serious efforts to respond to the degradation of their ocean dwelling places; we have little sense that we, too, have our being in and through the very oceans that are becoming increasingly unable to support whales. The subterranean depths of this crisis are remotely detectable in the perceived need to address global warming by the monstrously synecdochic call to save the polar bears. All of this speaks to our extreme alienation from our earth-selves. "Nature is finally not a 'wilderness' but a habitat, the best of habitats, a place where you can not only practice meditation or strive for a vision, but grow vegetables, play games with children, and drink wine with friends" (GSR, 294).[16]

Snyder's elemental language of mountains and rivers without end is not nostalgic—Zen is the call for mindfulness to the now and here—but rather language simultaneously of and in its awakening. Elemental earth language is Buddha Dharma language, now, here, awakening to the wilding of one's bioregion, including the voices of its decimated aboriginal inhabits, both human and nonhuman. Snyder, with his poet friends Philip Whalen and Allen Ginsberg, circumambulated Mt. Tamalpais in Marin County, across the Golden Gate Bridge from San Francisco, "circling and climbing—chanting—to show respect and clarify the mind, chanting, among other mantras and sūtras, the Dhāraṇī for Removing Disasters" (MR, 85). Disasters indeed! The elemental earth word—Tārā's endlessly wild sūtra language—pays attention (in the sense of the Buddha Dharma practice of *samyak-smṛti* or complete mindfulness) to the endless self-presentation of the Great Mind (our mind as mountains and rivers, mountains and rivers as our mind). It is a language of *grace*—"part of the first and last practice of the wild" (PW, 196), of gratitude for the gift of the Great Earth, a gift that is paradoxically desecrated if simply taken for granted. We do not have gratitude if we think that the Earth belongs to us; gratitude is an expression of the opposite: that we belong to the earth.

III

The reader enters the poetic cycle—*Mountains and Rivers without End* as an expression of the Great Earth—akin to the manner in which one enters into a reading of the *Endless Streams and Mountains* scroll itself. In both, the practice of reading transforms into its own meditative practice of the Wild:

> Clearing the mind and sliding in
>   to that created space
> a web of waters streaming over rocks. . . . (MR, 5)

One does not read the scroll merely in the way that an art historian does, exemplified by the aridly curatorial detective work of Sherman E. Lee and Wen Fong. (Their book is both valuable and sumptuous and its text is quite informative, but it is also comatose.) Sliding in after clearing the mind is an endless process, but so is the curatorial detective work as Susan Bush has also demonstrated.[17] The debates rage on as to when and how it was painted, how it should be read, and so on. This risks losing what makes these meditative scrolls even more powerful during the contemporary ecological crisis. Snyder recollects the Japanese artist HASEGAWA Saburo's (1906–1957) contention that "landscape paintings were for Zen as instructively and deeply Buddhist as the tankas and mandalas are for Tibetan Buddhism" (MR, 156).[18] The practice of reading the *shan-shui* scroll is to clear the mind in order to then find one's own internal landscape in the scroll's external landscape and to find in the scroll's external landscape one's own Great Earth mind.

In addition to reading across the length of the scroll's depiction of mountains, waters, and peoples and other creatures living in and through them, Snyder also studies some of the nine colophons that supplement the painting. The latter were added over the centuries when various owners of the scroll testified poetically that they had broken through to the painting and therefore attained the Great Mind that the mountains and rivers were expressing. "In a way the painting is not fully realized until several centuries of poems have been added" (MR, 161). (It is a little bit like the old Japanese art of *renga*, or linked poetry, in which various poets, each in their own singular way, display their attunement to the unfolding of a particular poetic event.) The painting (as well as the next link of a *renga*) can only be realized by those who in turn have been realized by it, much in the way that that Dōgen spoke of *ichibutsu-nibutsu*, one Buddha and two buddhas, that is, Buddha to Buddha communication. I seek to communicate my Buddha mind to you, the reader, the contemplator of the scroll, by awakening your own Buddha mind. It takes a Buddha to know a Buddha. Dharma communication requires techniques by which expression awakens the mind in order to be heard. If the mind is like a mirror, which can reflect everything, but it is covered in dust, no matter what I bring to the mirror, it reflects it in a dusty way. Merely holding forth on the Dharma does not clean the mirror. Communication in this respect is neither the transmission of information nor holding forth argumentatively, but rather cleaning the mirror or waking the mind of the interlocutor. The colophons testify to the awakening power of a particular painting and poem from the perspective of one's own awakening.

Indeed, as Wang Wen-wei[19] testifies in 1205, even the play of the ink (form) against the background of the silk (emptiness) attunes one to the miracle of "forests and springs": "Pale ink" [mountains, form] "on fine white silk" [emptiness, the background horizon that allows the foreground to manifest] (MR, 7). Days later, Li Hui added his doleful amazement that no one seems to be moved by the Great Earth (a poignant foreshadowing of the contemporary earth crisis):

> Everybody cheerful in these peaceful times.
> But I—why are my tastes so odd?
> I love the company of streams and boulders. (MR, 7)

Reading this scroll in the industrial and spiritual ruins of Cleveland, a place haunted by its spirits ("Old ghost ranges, sunken rivers, come again / stand by the wall and tell their tale"), Snyder then composes his own colophon.

Snyder explicitly gestures that his own poem is like a colophon being added to the scroll[20] by referencing his own lifting of the ink saturated brush ("grind the ink, wet the brush, unroll the / broad white space: / lead out and tip / the moist black line"). His *one bright pearl* reads:

Walking on walking,
                under foot   earth turns.

Streams and mountains never stay the same. (MR, 9, italics Snyder)

The whole poetic cycle itself is a variation of this colophon, each poem as singular as the colophons of the owners over the centuries, yet each held together by the mountains, rivers, and Great Earth. That the poems of *Mountains and Rivers without End* are in their own way also colophons is explicitly indicated at the end of the whole cycle, when Snyder frames all of the poems, forty years in their coming to be, by reiterating the colophon above and then finally putting away his brush:

The space goes on.
But the wet black brush
tip drawn to a point,
      lifts away. (MR, 154)

In between the opening and the closing of the earth-sūtra-scroll that is *Mountains and Rivers Without End*, there is not merely the transmission of wisdom as such, but in the clearing of the mind, there is also the critical opening of the heart. As Snyder quotes the *Avataṃsaka Sūtra*: "sentient beings are the roots of the tree-of awakening. The Bodhisattvas and the Buddhas are the flowers and fruits. Compassion is the water for the roots" (MR, 77). Mountains finally become buddhas—form as vehicles of Dharma—only with the advent of emptiness and its awakening of compassion. As the earth is subject to relentless mining, drilling, deforestation, and industrialization, emptiness and its flowing of compassion—Tārā as the walking of mountains—also becomes medicine for healing.

Rivers, flowing, the white of the scroll paper, all receiving form because they do not insist on a form of their own—"always new, same stuff . . . like each time was the first" (MR, 130)—are expressions of emptiness. The earth's waters, "reconstituted by respiration once every two million years or so" (MR,

139), join in an elemental dance with the sky. The kanji for emptiness (Jp. *kū* or Chinese *kōng*, 空) also means sky, and "The Blue Sky / is the land of OLD MAN MEDICINE BUDDHA / where the Eagle that Flies out of Sight / *flies*" (MR, 45). Flowing compassion, as endlessly deep as the sky is wide, its openness forming a horizon of visibility, is also the place, as a California Elder instructed Snyder, where the trembling hand of healing is itself healed by the guidance of "an eagle so high up in the sky as to be out of sight" (MR, 162). There is no healing without the transmission of the medicinal seeds of emptiness that root into the depths of the earth so as to open the tree to the endless expanse of the sky.

IV

One of the two epigrams that open *Mountains and Rivers Without End* is a lengthy quotation from "*Gabyō* [Painting of a Rice Cake]," where Dōgen makes the surprising claim that "Unsurpassed Enlightenment"—*anuttarā-samyak-saṃbodhi*, the unqualified consummation of the Buddha Way—"is a painting. The entire phenomenal universe and the empty sky are nothing but a painting. . . . Since this is so, there is no remedy for satisfying hunger other than a painted rice cake. Without painted hunger you never become a true person" (MR, xvii). To become a "true person," the Zen appropriation of a Daoist term to express a "great" or fully realized person, one must take seriously the problem of painting, and, by extension, the elementality of the poetic word.

In "*Busshō* [Buddha Nature]," when discussing Nāgārjuna, Dōgen claimed that we should "know that a true expression is not done by sound or form, and a true teaching has no particular shape" (S, 245). In this context, he recounts the skillful story (*upāya*) of Nāgārjuna's self-manifestation as the full-moon shape. Countless have tried to "paint this story" but "they have only painted the story with the tips of their brush" (S, 248). To really paint, you do not represent or mimic form, but you completely become a brush. Painting navigates the twin dangers of the fundamentalism of a preoccupation with form and the nihilism of *śūnyatā*-sickness.[21] "If people think that Nāgārjuna's manifestation of the full moon shape is merely a single circle, they truly see a painted rice cake [*gabyō*]. It is fooling others; such laughing kills people" (S, 248). When Nāgārjuna "became" a full moon, the point was not that he shifted his shape into the alternate shape of the full moon. The full moon (often associated with realization and awakening), rather, exposed

Nāgārjuna's shifting emptiness. His very body presented itself as *upāya*, as both the emptiness and the form of Nāgārjuna. The word medicine heals no one; the representation of the Buddha is not the emptiness of the Buddha. A painting (畫) of a rice cake is not nutritious. One cannot live on either images or concepts of food.

The image of the innutritious *gabyō* (painted rice cake) refers to a story in "*Keisei Sanshoku* [*Valley Sounds, Mountain Colors*]" about the great Buddhist scholar XIANGYAN Zhixian (died 898; Jp. KYŌGEN Chikan) who was challenged by GUISHAN Lingyou (Jp. ISAN Reiyū): "You are bright and knowledgeable. Say something about yourself before your parents were born, but don't use words learned from commentaries" (S, 87). The point is not to represent the Buddha conceptually or artistically, but to realize oneself and the Great Earth as the emptiness of the Buddha. Neither scholarship nor technical painting prowess realizes the living, empty ground of the Dharma. And so Xiangyan studied through the night, but failed: "Deeply ashamed, he burned the books and said, 'A painting of a rice cake does not satisfy hunger'" and so, in search of realization, he took up the preparation of actual food by becoming the monastery cook (S, 87).

The wily painted rice cake appears again in *Busshō* when Dōgen visited Ayuwang Mountain Guanli Monastery—home of the great Chinese *tenzo* (monastery cook) who taught Dōgen about the true meaning of practice and language—and was puzzled by one of its paintings and asked the guest coordinator Chenggui (Jp. Jōkei) what it was. Chenggui responded that it was a representation of Nāgārjuna manifesting in the shape of a full moon, to which Dōgen replied: "Truly it looks like a piece of painted rice cake" (S, 249). Chenggui laughed, but he "had no sword in his laughter and no ability to tear off the painted rice cake" (S, 249). Chenggui's laughter could not penetrate the husk of form so that heaven and earth could be born anew. Dōgen consequently counseled: "Never paint what cannot be painted. Paint straightforwardly what needs to be painted. Yet, [Nāgārjuna's] manifestation of the body in the shape of a full moon had never been painted" (S, 249). It had not been painted because the artist lacked the true Dharma eye of the imagination.

Yet in a later fascicle (*Gabyō*), explicitly dedicated to the problem of the painted rice cake, Dōgen prima facie seems to reverse his position. He clarifies that the point of practice is not to get beyond the painting of a rice cake: "There is no remedy for satisfying hunger other than a painted rice cake. Without painted hunger, you never become a true person" (S, 449). Indeed, in *upāya*, "all painted buddhas are actual buddhas" (S, 446) since we should "know that a painted rice cake is your face after your parents were born, your face before your parents were born." If tearing off the painted rice cake is abandoning the painting of the rice cake, this is nothing but *śūnyatā*-sickness, attachment to nothingness without seeing that "nothingness is shapeliness" (MR, 145). The *gabyō* is emptiness expressing itself as paint, which in turn expresses the elementality of paint. As Leonard Scigaj nicely puts it, "'Painted hunger' is the creative effort to achieve in the practice of writing the state of emptiness, the *śūnyatā* of hunger, through which one achieve enlightenment."[22] Hence, when the great YUNMEN Wenyan (Jp. Ummon Bun'en), was asked by a monk about going beyond buddhas and surpassing ancestors (i.e., not being caught in or attached to the form of the buddhas and the ancestors), he responded, "a sesame rice cake" (*Gabyō*, S, 447).

Art and science, the essay and song, are *upāya*, the mountains and rivers of the great earth of Tārā. The earth is not elsewhere—Dōgen often insists on the oneness of practice and realization (*shushō ittō*) because the Buddha is not waiting to come, but is already the elemental song of the earth "with no extra fog or mist" (S, 46). One does not practice in order eventually to reach realization. Realization is not elsewhere, either spatially or temporally. One's practice is one's ongoing realization, indeed the elemental practice of mountains and rivers and the Great Earth realization as such. The mind right now is Buddha (*soku-shin-ze-butsu*), but the anticipation of the Buddha as elsewhere, waiting to intervene upon oneself or the earth was what Dōgen unswervingly and vehemently dismissed as the *jinen gedō*, a heretical relationship to the Wild and the Great Earth. (Dōgen lived at a time in which the Dharma was believed to be in abeyance—the time of *mappō*—but this falsely implies that the Dharma is somewhere else and sometime else than here at the present moment.) In the sūtra of the earth—its appreciative study, its artistic invocation—we find our ongoing elemental realization. The earth is a great painting because, reciprocally, a great painting awakens our elemental awareness of the earth just as the earth, on the cusp of its eclipse, sings and paints and speaks itself.

V

In the *Shōbōgenzō* fascicle "*Baika* [Plum Blossoms]," Dōgen once again turns to the poetic word of his late and great Chinese teacher, RUJING Tiantong (whom the Japanese call Nyojō Tendō), with whom Dōgen had studied in China and with whom he experienced his celebrated libratory "falling and casting away of body and mind [*shinjin datsuraku*]." Dōgen, himself a fine poet,[23] makes an astonishing claim about Rujing's poetry and likens it to what in the TANAHASHI edition of the *Shōbōgenzō* is translated as *painting* (畫, a kanji read variously as *ga* or *e*, a sketch, stroke, or mark, but it can also be read as suggestive of an image, as in painting, drawing, picture):

> Rujing said:
> The original face is beyond birth and death.
> Spring in plum blossoms enters into a painting.
> When you paint spring, do not paint willows, plums, peaches, or apricots—just paint spring. To paint willows, plums, peaches, or apricots is to paint willows, plums, peaches, or apricots. It is not yet painting spring.
> It is not that spring cannot be painted, but aside from Rujing, there is no one in India or China who has painted spring. He alone was a sharp-pointed brush that painted spring.
> This spring is spring in the painting as it enters into a painting. He does not use other means, but lets plum blossoms initiate spring. He lets spring enter into a painting and into a tree. This is skillful means [*upāya*]. (S, 588–589)

Dōgen, using his characteristic hyperbole ("aside from Rujing, there is no one in India or China who has painted spring"), insists that painterly or poetic images *are not representations*. Painting does not merely reproduce the forms of Nature with either word or ink. When Rujing marks spring's entry into a "painting," Rujing himself had to become "a sharp-pointed brush." It did not suffice just to use the brush. Rujing does not paint spring as an object for a painter-subject, but rather "lets plum blossoms initiate spring." They can only initiate spring if Rujing forgets himself as either a subject or an object and experiences himself as no longer separate from spring's self-presentation and, indeed, from the Wild's ongoing self-presentation.

One could say that the self-presentation of the Wild as painting can in part be expressed through the double meaning of the English word "realization." As NISHITANI Keiji explained his phrase the "self-awareness of reality":

> I mean both our becoming aware of reality and, at the same time, the reality realizing itself in our awareness. The English word "realize,"

with its twofold meaning of "actualize" and "understand," is particularly well suited to what I have in mind here, although I am told that its sense of "understand" does not necessarily connote the sense of reality coming to actualization in us. Be that as it may, I am using the word to indicate that our ability to perceive reality means that reality realizes (actualizes) itself in us; that this in turn is the only way that we can realize (appropriate through understanding) the fact that reality is so realizing itself in us; and that in so doing the self-realization of reality itself takes place.[24]

Rujing realizes that the ongoing event of his self is inseparable from the self-realization of the Wild and that the self-realization of the Wild is inseparable from his own ongoing self-realization. He realizes (understands) that Rujing as the Wild and the Wild as Rujing are inseparable from reality in each moment realizing itself (becoming real and understanding itself as the ongoing self-presentation of the real). "Painting spring" realizes not only spring, but also self-realization as such. The constructed image expresses the self-presentation of the Wild directly, rather than confusing it lopsidedly with one of its forms. In painting and the poetic word the artist lets the Wild say itself anew, here and now. One can even detect a hint of this in the Latinate English word "Nature" itself. The Latin *natura* does not merely name the totality of all natural objects, but also speaks of their "birth" (from *natus* "born," pp. of *nasci* "to be born"). Using a distinction in Spinoza that Schelling in his *Naturphilosophie* held dear even as he critically transformed it, one could say that most of us study and occupy ourselves with *natura naturata* [literally, nature natured], already born nature, nature in its having already become what it is. It is much harder to realize *natura naturans* [literally, nature naturing, the Wilding wilding], nature in the event of its self-presentation. Yet the presentations of nature, nature as it has appeared, are inseparable from the event of its appearing, from the passageless-passage (*kyōryaku*) that is the natality of nature.[25]

To be more direct: Dōgen is claiming that spring is not to be confused with *any particular form of spring*. Although April may breed lilacs out of the dead land, as Eliot famously lamented, spring is not lilacs; it is different from the content of any particular form that we associate with spring while at the same time having no independent standing of its own. To associate spring with particular springtime occurrences is to mistake spring for those occurrences. "To paint willows, plums, peaches, or apricots is to paint willows, plums, peaches, or apricots. It is not yet painting spring." Spring is not the idea of spring as a definition or delimitation of the event of spring. Spring is not a being, but rather an experience of time by which we understand beings in a certain manner. Spring is an event that, while expressing itself as forms, has no particular form of its own and is attached to none of its self-expressions. Were all plants to disappear, spring itself would not disappear.

Moreover, spring is a way of understanding these forms, even form as such. "Painting spring" cannot be accomplished by representing it as any of the typical forms of spring. The fruits of "painting spring" must rather express the Dharma directly. The verb "express" itself is an attempt to express what Dōgen calls *dōtoku*. The first of the two kanji that comprise *dōtoku* is *dō*, which is the Japanese reading of the Chinese character for Dao (道), the great pivot at the heart of the "ten thousand things," the "myriad beings," that is to say, the absolute nothingness that actively expresses itself as all beings. *Dō* also has a secondary valence, namely, to say or to express, with or without words. *Toku* (得), on the other hand, is to be able or capable of doing something as well as to attain or grasp something. It is quite literally in this case the ability to speak, which we can here interpret as the attainment of expressivity, which is more fundamentally the attainment or grasp of Dao in terms of the ability to express Dao, to say the unsayable, to realize the soundless sound and the formless form in word and works, that is, to be able to express Dao without naming it, without snaring it in either words or works. (The Dao and the Dharma can be "expressed" by these names, but these names, or any other names, do not capture the Dao or Dharma.)[26]

Although the poetic word expresses the Wild without representing the Wild, it is not helpful to interpret this as arguing that the Wild is simply unsayable, that it evades language altogether. It eludes determination because it is not something that can be determined. It eludes representation because there is nothing to represent. "The scale of the mind cannot be known by thinking and discernment" (S, 59) Dōgen tells us. It originates and animates myths and dreams and poems (Tārā, the trickster Coyote, the trickster Raven, etc.), but this is not to say that myths, dreams, and poems are just lies and that the truth in itself defies any expression. Snyder dismisses this as mere "mischief" that "gets people off the hook too easily" (NH, 43):

> If you have an understanding and cannot express it, then your understanding is not yet complete. The act of expressing clarifies your understanding of it. However, the nature of that expression may not

be clear and transparent to everybody, which is why Zen literature is not easy to follow. But that's what it is. So the person who has a Zen eye can understand it. (NH, 43)

The problem of expression also allows us to appreciate Dōgen's final claim in the passage with which we began this section. When Rujing "lets spring enter into a painting and into a tree," Dōgen calls this "skillful means" (*upāya* in Sanskrit and *hōben* in Japanese). All art, including the poetic word, is *upāya*. In the Mahāyāna traditions, *upāya* speaks to the capacity to make something true heard in the terms and conventions of the prevailing mind-set.[27]

In the third chapter of the *Lotus Sūtra*, for example, the Buddha explains *upāya* to Śāriputra through a parable—itself a kind of skillful or expedient mean to express the problem of skillful or expedient means as such. Śāriputra is asked to imagine a man of great wealth whose house has caught on fire and although he knows that he can easily escape, his many sons are so absorbed in their games (attachments) that they cannot see the fire raging all around them. When the father tries to alert his sons to the problem, they are "unalarmed and unafraid . . . for they do not even know what a 'fire' is, or what a 'house' is, or what it means to 'lose' anything."[28] What to do? The father devises an expedient but technically incorrect mean (i.e., it does not aspire to be an accurate or responsible representation). He promises them the rare toys outside the house that the sons have always desired. The sons, their hearts aflame with desire, rush from the house. The Buddha asks Śāriputra if the father is guilty of telling a lie and Śāriputra already sees that the father has put his sons on the path to realization, even though they do not yet understand it. For the Buddha, this means that the teaching of the Three Vehicles was merely expedient means "in order to entice the beings" (LS, 64), to turn them eventually from their dull minds to a direct experience of the truth already concealed within these nonetheless expressive words.[29] It is a saying in which saying as such comes to be heard. One comes to see that the Buddha was already in the burning house itself. That is to say, the burning house (the first noble truth of *duḥkha* or the stress of life out of whack) drives us to the Buddha Dharma, but the latter comes to be seen as expressing itself as all beings, even the burning house that first appeared wholly and irreconcilably opposed to Buddha Dharma. The problem was not the burning house per se, but rather our own inability to see. The burning house was our own ignorance (*avidyā*, literally, nonseeing).

This is a critical issue in how we read the *Lotus Sūtra*. There is a tradition that holds that this text was written to consolidate Mahāyāna into a single system of teaching. This would contradict the very idea of *upāya*, which implies that there are no teachings in themselves, no doctrine that somehow exists in itself, which is repackaged in culturally specific ways. The consolidation reading of the *Lotus Sūtra* assumes that there is master doctrine that one cunningly translates into more easily digestible forms for one's dull students, relegating *upāya* to the craft of bringing others around to one's own point of view. But the Dharma is not a dogma nor is it *sensu stricto* a metaphysical view. *Upāya* does not seek to brainwash students into upholding a doctrine or to convince students of a philosophical perspective. *Upāya* is the art of opening the true Dharma eye. William LaFleur,[30] in contrast, in his classic *The Karma of Words*, called *upāya* "self-reflexive allegory; that is, their trajectory of discourse behaves like a boomerang." Like the Dharma itself in the *Lotus Sutra*, *upāya* narratives are "characterized by 'the absolute identity [or equality] of their beginning and end.'"[31]

Or as Taigen Dan Leighton concurs, *upāya* in the *Lotus Sutra* embodies "the awakening aspect of the phenomenal world, omnipresent, at least in potentiality, in all concrete particulars."[32] Leighton has a lovely appreciation of Dōgen's understanding of this aspect of the *Lotus Sutra*, citing jōdō 49 of the *Eihei Kōroku* where Dōgen confesses that it is no longer he who is teaching the monks. "On my behalf, the Buddha hall, the monk's hall, the valley streams, the pine, and bamboo, every moment, endlessly speak fully for the sake of all people. Have you all heard it or not?"[33] *Upāya* enables one to hear that all of the places of the Great Earth are in their own manner *upāya*, all speaking with the long broad tongue of the Buddha.

The point of hearing and studying a particular *upāya* is not to become attached to it as an end in itself. "Have you all heard it or not?" If you have heard it, you do not just have the poetic word, or the myth, or the *upāya* parable. You have the Buddha at the heart of all manifestation, whether it be avocadoes or poems about avocadoes. If you have not heard it, your practice is poor, that is, "you do not keep the five precepts." *Upāya* itself always runs the risk of losing the freshness of the now and here and becoming didactic. Snyder, for example, laments the sedimentation that has it occurred in a lot of Japanese Zen because of its professionalization (its expert capacity to deliver a known product). "The Japanese Zen world of the last few centuries has become so expert and professional in the matter of strict training that it has lost to a great extent the capacity to surprise itself" (PW, 162).

The rigorous adherence to form and training eventually allows the freedom of emptiness as the heart of the form. "This is the surprise of discovering oneself needing no self, one with the work, moving in disciplined ease and grace" (PW, 158), much like Zhuangzi's famous Cook Ding and the effortless effort that was the grace of having mastered the Way of the meat cleaver. Lord Wen-hui was amazed by Ding's effortless mastery, which transcended mere skill (how to do things) and embodied the Dao. This is the paradox at the heart of freedom and spontaneity (what Zhuangzi called *ziran*, the "thus so," or spontaneous Way of the Wild): that it is hard work to get beyond oneself. Or as Snyder's Zen teacher ODA Sessō Rōshi admonished everyone: "The perfect way is without difficulty. Strive hard" (PW, 160)!

In this sense, *upāya* communicates indirectly and freshly, expressing the Dharma through the non-duality of emptiness and form. Although the Dharma can only express itself as forms, it has no original form of its own and hence the Dharma and the Buddha are already present in *upāya*. They are not elsewhere. *Upāya* is not pointing beyond itself, but rather into itself. The Dharma manifests, however, when it is not confused with the words and images that express it, but rather when it is experienced directly as the living emptiness within forms. The poetic word is *upāya* when it expresses directly the emptiness (or "original face") of form.

The problem of the emptiness of form is not unknown in some modern European art. For a dramatic example, one need only look at *Der Blaue Reiter* movement in Munich in the early Twentieth Century. The "original face" of form is what Wassily Kandinsky famously called the problem of the spiritual [*das Geistige*], which he considered to be the problem of art as such. In his essay "*Über die Formfrage* [On the Question of Form]," which appeared in the group's famous Almanac, Kandinsky articulated the problem of form:

> Form is always temporal, i.e., relative, for it is nothing more than the means necessary today through which the present revelation makes itself heard . . . *Form is the outer expression of the inner content* . . . We should never make a god out of form. We should struggle for form only as long as it serves as *a means of expression for the inner sound*. Therefore, we should not look for salvation in *one* form only.[34]

The inner content of art is not in itself a form nor can it be contained as content. Artistic form is, to borrow the insight from Mahāyāna, empty. From this perspective, art is not the mastery of form for the sake of form and in this sense art is not the imitation of Nature if by that one means that one is called to represent what Nature has first presented. One needs somehow to see through form in order to get beyond form. One somehow has to see the invisible. *"Necessity creates form.* Fish that live at great depths have no eyes" (QF, 150). To see without eyes is to see freely, not in the sense of granting one's own ego free license to do whatever it wants, but rather to participate in the sovereignty of Nature's own imagination, that is, in the freedom at the heart of the coming to be of form. This freedom is not found in myself because I, like the artwork, am a product of this freedom.

In order to produce, or even appreciate, art, one cannot stop with its form.

> In daily life we would rarely find a man who will get off the train at Regensburg when he wants to go to Berlin. In spiritual life, getting off at Regensburg is a rather common occurrence. Sometimes even the engineer does not want to go on, and all the passengers get off at Regensburg. How many who sought God stopped at a carved figure! How many who searched for art were arrested at a form that an artist had used for her own purposes, be it Giotto, Raphael, Dürer, or Van Gogh! (QF, 153)

Only in becoming the fish without eyes that somehow sees can one attune oneself to the event of presentation. *"The future* can be received only through freedom" (QF, 187). As Schelling had shown a century earlier, this freedom can already be detected in the word for the imagination, namely, *Einbildungskraft*, the power (*Kraft*) of the one (in itself nothing) coming into form or image (*Bild*). The imagination is the plastic force of nature, much in the way that Catherine Malabou has so effectively deployed the problem of plasticity.[35] Its freedom is the sovereignty of coming into form.

This problem was even more acutely present in the work of Kandinsky's colleague, Paul Klee, whose famous epitaph was taken from some lines in Leopold Zahn's 1920 book, *Paul Klee: Leben, Werk, Geist*, where Zahn recounts the story of Zhuangzi who, under the force of the Dao, was at home with both the living and the dead. As evidence of Klee's attunement to the Dao, Zahn cited Klee's own self-understanding: "I cannot be understood at all on this earth. For I live as much with the dead as with the unborn. Somewhat closer to the heart of creation than usual. But not nearly close enough."[36] And what was it to be somewhat closer to the heart of creation? It was the detachment from the ego-self and its passions and the awakening to the creativity of Nature. "Do I emanate warmth? Coolness? For there is nothing to discuss beyond all fervor.

I am most pious at the greatest distance [*Am fernsten bin ich am frömmsten*]."[37] Such piety allowed Klee to be present to the self-presentation of Nature as art. "Form shall never and nowhere be considered as a result, as the end, but as genesis, as becoming, as essence. As appearance, form is an evil and dangerous ghost."[38] If form does not express spiritual life, it is nothing but the haunting return of the dead. (Not in the sense of the dead telling their stories, as they do for Snyder, but rather the deadening of one's practice.)

Dōgen was not advocating for the annihilation of form and the elevation of emptiness as an exclusive disjunction. The excessive concern with emptiness is the nihilistic and pernicious Zen *śūnyatā*-sickness (what Hakuin derides as *kūbyō*), as if one were evacuating the concrete and making some kind of headlong descent into pure—that is, merely abstract—emptiness. Art is the nonseparation of form and emptiness, not the nihilistic and reactive emptying out of all forms. NISHITANI Keiji, following the great Rinzai Zen reformer HAKUIN Ekaku (1686–1768), warned against this. "The 'solid frozen all sameness of the *Tathātā*,' the 'ice of the one dharma nature,' the 'ice covered absolute one or absolute identity,' etc. refer to those higher attachments to self and law that lie hidden at the level beyond ordinary attachments to self and law." Only when one breaks through this hidden source of narcissism, when the "Great Mirror Wisdom" tears one asunder, does the "infinite fragrance" of life emerge.[39]

The "infinite fragrance" of life emerges in what Nishitani called the "field of *śūnyatā* [*kū no ba*]," which is "not that the self and things are empty but that emptiness is the self and things" (RN, 138). This *ba* (場) is not some place, here or elsewhere, for there "is literally no place to stand" (RN, 15). It is not here in the sense that it is not any object, present or otherwise. It is not elsewhere in the sense that there is no place that it is not. Looking for it elsewhere, Dōgen warned us, is like running all over the place looking for your head or traveling south in search of the North Star. For Nishitani, it is the background which is nothing in itself, but which allows form to foreground itself much as the empty sky allows form to emerge.[40] This field is the standpoint that transforms the experience of form into something no longer fundamentally formal, no longer a representation, but rather as something more intimate, vital, and temporally dynamic. It is to see in form the soundless sound and to hear in form the formless form.[41] From the standpoint of *śūnyatā*, form does not disappear, but rather one experiences *śūnyatā* in its ongoing self-presentation as forms. It is *śūnyatā* as (*soku*) this form. The *soku* is a kind of pivot in which in each moment there is neither emptiness nor its opposite, form—these in themselves are nothing but unhealthy abstractions.

Rather, *śūnyatā*, which in itself opposes this or any form, expresses itself right now and right here *as this form*.

In an essay, "Emptiness and Sameness [*Kū to Soku*]," on the relationship between *śūnyatā* (*kū*) and this "as [*soku*]," Nishitani asks us to consider looking at a beautiful *chawan* (tea bowl):

> The shape is the factor that gives the tea bowl the name "tea bowl." It has the form of a utensil made to drink water hot and cold water, with a hollow and an opening to contain other liquids. . . . Our sensorial perception discerns the object in front of us as a tea bowl by its shape. In our general daily experience, the object in front of us receives the connotation of the general concept known as "tea bowl" by its form."[42]

Indeed, the *chawan* as a particular instantiation of the general idea of a *chawan* is where we begin. We begin by recognizing *what* it is. "At the beginning was the form . . . " (ES, 215). Yet the *chawan* is not merely either the idea or the image of a *chawan*; it also came to be *imagined* as a *chawan*. But what does this say about the imagination? It mediates the concept (you can imagine the form of a tea bowl) and the perception (you can recognize what you see), but it is nonetheless "basically different from both." If I know what a *chawan* is, that is, if I understand the idea of a *chawan*, I can also conjure up in my imagination an image of a particular *chawan*. I can see a *chawan* and recognize it by its idea. In this way the imagination can hold together idea and image, but the imagination derives neither from the practice of entertaining ideas nor from sensuously intuiting things. It does not first and foremost perceive, cognize, or recognize; it creates. It is the coming into being of something that we may then attempt to cognize and develop the habits by which to make it recognizable. In its coming to being, the image is not being perceived as already there, but as something newly imagined. The imagination "freely creates images" (ES, 216) and "sensorial intuition and perception create a non-given figure."

As an example, Nishitani recounts a poetic image from a Meiji era monk by the name of Tairyū, who burned some incense during the festival commemorating the enlightenment of Śākyamuni Buddha, and imaginatively composed these words:

> With the pupils of my eyes blinded, I look at the universe.
> The frosty wind pierces my bones: how cold!

Dust on the path back to my house.
In the snow the fragrance of plum blossoms hits the tip of my nose.
(ES, 216)

The imagination in its particular mode of perception neither recognizes nor represents. In order to see, it has to see in another way: "With the pupils of my eyes blinded, I look at the universe." Eyes that no longer see objects, either in an intellectual or sensorial mode, can see imaginatively, that is, see an image in its mode of origination. It is to "see" as Kandinsky "saw": "fish that live at great depths have no eyes." The imagination is sovereign, an "unhindered" movement, "the opening of the world as the 'one' in the expression 'one = many' or in the world as 'opening'" (ES, 201). This opening is "absolute" (ES, 201). Hence, the opening of the world is equal to "emptiness," and as such an empty world is "nonadherent" (ES, 202). This last term, "nonadherence," translates the important Zen term, *mu-ichi-motsu*, 無一物, literally, not a single thing, owning nothing whatsoever, having nothing to cling or attach to (and hence a lack of substance in all things, not a thing that all things are).

This phrase recalls the third line of the famous poem by the Sixth Patriarch, Dajian Huineng (Jp. Daikan Enō), which attempts to undo any clinging even to the practice of polishing the mirror of the original self. The poetic image of a mirror is the *upāya* by which I might experience Linji's "true self with no rank," but it is not *what* the true or original self is. When Hongren, the Fifth Patriarch, sponsored a poetry contest to locate his successor, Shenxiu (Jinshū for the Japanese) composed a gatha likening the body and the mind to two recognizable images: a bodhi tree and a mirror, respectively. They should be polished to keep the dust of the mundane world from polluting their clarity.[43] Huineng's poem cut more sharply to the heart of the matter: He denied that the body reduces to the image of a bodhi tree or the mind to a mirror. "Originally there is not one thing" (ZS, 25). As such, it reduces to no image; it eludes final determination and cannot be captured in any definition (it is not "one").[44] Like water, it can take any form, but it has no form of its own and, originally not being one thing, not even water, no thing can hinder it. In our example, emptiness is (in the sense of *soku*) this particular *chawan*, but in itself it is originally not one thing; in itself it is nothing whatsoever, the "original face" of the *chawan*. Like one's original face before one's parents were born, emptiness is the unimaginable ground of the imagination and the dreamtime. For Snyder, one could also say the original face is the depth relation of every place to the Great Earth itself.

VI

The poetic word is indispensible during the ecological crisis, and, as such, it cannot be separated from dreaming and the dreamtime. If ever there seemed to be an antithesis to the sober rationality of science, it would be dreams. Science yields, beyond any personal preferences, to what things are, but dreams seem like the arbitrary, unmotivated and senseless expression of the mind when it is in the off position.

In his profound new book, *Waking, Dreaming, Being*, Evan Thompson provocatively demonstrates that when dreaming, the mind is not switched off. Even when falling asleep—the so-called hypnogogic state, the state leading into *hypnos* or sleep—the mind is not shutting down, but it is doing something that has some important features in common with meditation. If the waking mind tries to shut itself off to go to sleep, it cannot. The more we try to take credit for sleeping as something that we actively do, the more we cannot sleep. We toss and turn, our thoughts agitated, as we try to tell ourselves to sleep. One rather falls asleep, reminiscent in some ways of Dōgen's *shinjin datsuraku*, or casting away and falling away of body and mind. As one is drifting off to sleep, the mind fills with all sorts of images, but they are not images for which one can take credit. In a sense, one is experiencing one's mind as not one's *own* mind. "Two key features mark the hypnogogic state—a slackening of the sense of self and a spellbound identification of consciousness with what it spontaneously imagines."[45]

In lucid dreaming, that is, when I become aware of myself dreaming as I am dreaming, who is this witness? It cannot see itself; rather it becomes aware of itself precisely as awareness. It is a dreaming self, not a dream ego. At the level of brain activity, brain-imaging studies of lucid dreamers do not reveal a single part of the brain activating, as if the self were waking up while dreaming and looking at a dream as a subject looks at an object. "Rather, lucid dreaming—like all modes of consciousness—reflects large-scale and distributed patterns of brain activity."[46] Or when I experience an out-of-body experience in dreaming, it is not because I am becoming detached from my body. It is rather how I am experiencing the slackening of my ordinary, deeply situated mind and its habitual orientation. Thompson extends his inquiry even into deep sleep and death as modes in which the ego-mind widens into what Snyder calls the "Great Mind" (MR, 73).

When the *Diamond Sūtra* famously refers to beings as a dream, an illusion, a bubble, and a shadow, or when Nāgārjuna in the *Mūlamadhyamaka-kārikā* likens everything to a dream, this does not mean that it is *my* dream or that everything is an idealistic representation of consciousness. To the extent that it is helpful to think of it as a dream, it is a dream without a dreamer and it exudes the wildness and spontaneity that is already evident in the hypnogogic state. In a sense we could say that calling everything a dream is like calling everything *upāya*. The point is not to become more somnolent, but more awake, more conscious.

The power of the dream and dreamtime is a prevalent feature in Snyder's poetry and it is a critical aspect of *Mountains and Rivers Without End*. In order to access the mythic, either in hearing the stories that belong to a particular place or in creatively adding to them, you have to "go through the gateway of the dream"[47] as Robert Hass tells us. For David Abram, what dreaming and the dreamtime open up in both our minds and the Great Earth itself is "Deep Time," that is, a "kind of depth, ambiguous and metamorphic. Indeed, it is a sense of both the past and the future not as dimensions that reside somewhere else, but as realms that are hidden, secretly, within the depths of the present moment. A sense of time as depth."[48] Practice is not the way toward a future goal, something along a temporal path that is there, in the future, waiting about as the anticipated destination. The oneness of practice and realization (*shushō-ittō*) insists that the Buddha is not to come, but always already at the depths of each and every present moment. "This present moment that lives on to become long ago" sings Snyder (PM, 67). For Dōgen, ABE Masao, tells us, "there is no time that is not the right time" (SD, 70).

In dreaming the wildness of these depths manifests. One loses the poetic word in order to find it, throws it away in hope that it returns on its own terms. This is how Snyder understands the place aware attunement of his poetry, words emerging from the meeting of place and the wild depths of the Great Earth.

How Poetry Comes to Me

It comes blundering over the
Boulders at night, it stays
Frightened outside the
Range of my campfire
I go to meet it at the
Edge of the light. (NN, 361)

Meeting the poetic word "at the edge of the night" does not mean that one desensitizes oneself to place. In the many dreams in *Mountains and Rivers without End*, the concrete does not disappear into vague generalities about the Great Earth. It is the opposite: the Great Earth attunes one more precisely and mindfully, but also more creatively and openly, to the concrete. The latter retains its freshness, its aptness, and its capacity to surprise. This is at the heart of *upāya* as well as the indigenous myths of Turtle Island.[49]

This surprise is the movement of expansion—of becoming more than one thought one was. Snyder's cat in Berkeley, Genji, catches a grey bird; after Snyder puts it out of its misery "it swelled" and "became a woman, and I was embracing her" ("Journeys," MR, 54). The dying grey bird is also Tārā. This dynamic is clearest in the beautiful and poignant poem, "The Elwha River" in which Snyder dreams that he is a very pregnant and quite vulnerable teenage girl waiting for a boyfriend who may never arrive. She then sat down in a class and wrote an essay about "What I Just Did," only to receive a C– because her teacher resented that she was no longer a man (MR, 32).

Although the history of Buddhism has by and large utterly failed women, as well as gay, lesbian, and transgender people, Snyder's dream resonates with discourses found in the *Lotus Sūtra* and the *Vimalakīrti Sūtra*. Mañjuśrī in the twelfth chapter of the *Lotus Sūtra*, for example, defends the daughter of the dragon king, recounting the *upāya* of a seven-year-old girl who becomes fully awakened (and that she is the daughter of a dragon also aligns her with the maligned domain of the nonhuman). "Her eloquence has no obstructions, and she is compassionately mindful of the beings if they were her babies. Her merits are perfect" (LS, 199). Upon meeting her, Śāriputra is scandalized. "This is hard to believe. What is the reason? A woman's body is filthy, it is not a Dharma-receptacle. How can you attain unexcelled bodhi" (LS, 200–201)? The dragon girl proves Śāriputra wrong. In putting Śāriputra's discrimination in its place, the dragon girl instantly turns into a man (LS, 201). This, of course, has led some readers to conclude that the male form remains the requisite vehicle for awakening, although this fails to take into account that she was already fully awakened before she made sport of Śāriputra. In the seventh chapter of the *Vimalakīrti Sūtra*, Śāriputra the misogynist is even more thoroughly schooled.[50] Śāriputra asks the goddess to change out of her form, but the goddess responds that a woman does not reduce to a mere form. "All things are just the same—they have no fixed form."[51]

The gender fluidity of Snyder's dream resonates with his sense of reincarnation: we have been and will become all beings. To care for all beings is to care for yourself. To care for yourself is to care for all beings. In doing so, always err on the side of the marginalized and vulnerable. This is in part why Tārā chose to be a woman:

> "Those who wish to attain supreme enlightenment
> in a man's body are many . . .
> therefore may I,
> > *until this world is emptied out,*
> serve the needs of beings
> with my body of a woman." (MR, 110–11)

This is not to say that Tārā regards bodies as interchangeable or that because all things are ultimately empty, we should ignore their concrete tribulations. Each way of being a body is singular. The decimation of species in the Sixth Great Extinction is not the loss of a large quantity of generic bodies. It is the loss of singular forms of life that in their singularity are precious. Hence, in recalling the dream, the Elwha River, whose bridge was redolent with redwood, Snyder does not recall that he is really a man but rather that "there are no redwoods north of southern / Curry County, Oregon" (MR, 32). Recently, the Elwha River had its dams removed and it once again flows freely to the Strait of Juan de Fuca from Olympic National Park. It was the only river in Washington State that once supported the seasonal return of all of the major species of salmon. We dream that they may once again find their way back. May all beings flourish.

PART II

Turtle Island

3

Place
(Land and Sea, Earth and Sky)

Black Coyote saw the whole world
In Wovoka's empty hat
—"The Hump-backed Flute Player" (MR, 83)

I

Although Snyder has traveled broadly across the earth, he is always mindful of place, including the fact that he was born and raised and spent much of his life on the West Coast of Turtle Island (Northern California, Oregon, and Washington).[1] In all of his writing, from wherever he may be writing, he attends to its place, but that does not mean that he merely rehearses the official account of *where* that is. As Carl Bielefeldt tells us, he wanders in the tradition of Xuanzang (who traveled from China to India in the seventh century on a seventeen-year pilgrimage to bring the Dharma and more than six-hundred sūtras back) and Kokop'ele (the humpbacked flute player traveler found in the petroglyphs in the Southwest of Turtle Island) in attempting to sacralize the land by sowing it with his songs.[2]

This chapter inquires into the *problem of place* as a critical dimension of ecological philosophy in Snyder's work. We habitually but falsely imagine ourselves to be *in* a place, but Snyder, who "never forgot, or left, that first ground, the 'where' of our 'who are we?'" (PS, 184), counters that not only *are* we a place, but we are also the practice of that place, or, as Dōgen articulated it: "When you find your place where you are, practice occurs" (quoted in PW, 27). We do not merely adopt a practice as if it were some set of elective actions. We *are* the depths of our practices and those depths express our interdependent being as a bioregion, our *"spirit of what it was to be there"*

(PS, 185). *What is this libratory, wild, Great Earth-centered practice of ourselves as place?*

I develop this question by attending to the place that Snyder, following the Haudenosaunee or Iroquois Confederacy, called Turtle Island, and which we currently occupy as North America. "People live on it without knowing what it is or where they are. They live on it literally like invaders" (RW, 69). I seek to "*dis*cover" (RW, 69) Turtle Island, that is, attempt to remove some of the obfuscation of imperial ideology, first by turning to Melville's *Moby-Dick* as an avenue by which to explore the nature of the creation and occupation of this space; I then attempt to retrieve what is obscured by these monomaniacal, destructive, and "stingy"[3] practices of place.

II

Melville gifts us with one of the truly profound contemplations of the place-specific problem by which Turtle Island came to be a very different kind of place and a very different kind of people. Like his contemporary Thoreau, Melville meditated on the problem of this place at the site of its eclipse. As the American poet Charles Olson tells us in his singular study of *Moby-Dick*: "Melville had a way of reaching back through time until he got history pushed back so far he turned time into space. . . . We are the last 'first' people. We forget that. We act big, misuse our land, ourselves."[4] Melville "sought prime" and it is from the primacy of pure space, in his case, the placelessness of the sea, that he sought to articulate, on the eve of its disappearance, a new version of the ancient relationship to the Wild, to "make a myth, *Moby-Dick*, for a people of Ishmaels" (CMI, 15).

Just as Thoreau's experiments with solitude in his cabin on Walden Pond revealed to him that "the mass of men lead lives of quiet desperation," Melville loosens the hold of the New World's fixed, self-referential, and self-serving sense of place, which he associated with the unreflective and self-interested habits by which we have put the land to our disposal. He does this by carefully detailing life at sea aboard the whaling ship the Pequod, filled with crewmembers that represent the great genetic and cultural diversity of our species and which is presumably named after the decimated Pequot tribe, an Algonquian-speaking people who had primarily lived in what is now Connecticut. Like the country itself, the Pequod is a place that houses great diversity and democratic promise, but which is also haunted by the decimation that it had wrought on other ways of life as it unilaterally established its own ways of life.

Melville's novel enacts a breakdown (and thereby a breakthrough) of the habituated stinginess of the New World ideology of space by unleashing at its heart the senseless but overwhelming force of the great *outlandish* sea. "No mercy, no power but its own controls it. Panting and snorting like a mad battle steed that has lost its rider, the masterless ocean overruns the globe" (chapter 58, The Brit).[5] The seas, and their sublime symbol, the great white whale Moby Dick, burst through and undo the hold of routinized and habituated land-oriented living and thinking—what Deleuze and Guattari, great admirers of Melville, have called the "territorialized." The sea deterritorializes, exposing openness and sovereignty at the depths of space.

Ahab ruinously helms the Pequod. Although he is firmly in control of the ship, he has lost control of himself and has become a howling, monomaniacal animal, obsessed with the white whale. With the exception of his strange and unexpected friendship with the little African-American boy Pip, who had lost his mind after falling into the wide-open expanse of the sea, Ahab constitutively can see nothing beyond his quest. Anything else that he might be disappears as his obsession commandeers him. In this sense, I would here depart from Deleuze's extreme emphasis on Ahab's radical alteration:

> Of what is Captain Ahab guilty? Of having chosen Moby Dick, the white whale, instead of obeying the law of the group of fishermen, according to which all whales are fit to hunt. In that lies Ahab's demonic element, his treason, his relationship with Leviathan—this choice of object which engages him in a whale-becoming himself.[6]

This is to some extent true. Ahab has lost himself, but not merely because he becomes the leviathan, but rather because he is fixated on subjecting its power to himself, much like Saint Augustine, who in *Confessions* realized that he had lived as if it were he who was God. Or as Snyder cites Dōgen: "when the ten thousand things come forward and verify you, that is enlightenment but when you go forward and verify the ten thousand things, that is delusion."[7] This is Ahab's delusion, a delusion that vanquishes the Pequod and Turtle Island. Ahab sacrifices the Great Earth to become himself, but in becoming himself, he must subject all that contests him, as if he could conquer death and senselessness itself. He does not so much become the leviathan but rather the one who must at all costs *attempt to become the whale* and to make the otherwise humiliating power of the sea his own. It is in this sense that Olson spoke so precisely about Ahab in terms of

> the Roman feeling about the world. It is his, to dispose of. He strides it, with possession of it. His property. Has he not conquered it with his machines? He bends its resources to his will. The pax of legions? the Americanization of the world. Who else is lord? . . .
>
> OVER ALL, hate—huge and fixed upon the imperceptible. Not man but all the hidden forces that terrorize man is assailed by the American Timon. That HATE, extra-human, involves his Crew, and Moby Dick drags them to their death as well as Ahab to his, a collapse of a hero through the solipsism that brings down a world. (CMI, 73)

Ahab, now the extra-human—the one who would be leviathan—suffers from a hyperbolic variation of Macbeth's tragic ambition, "the solipsism that brings down a world." Before the immensity of space he becomes the one who must be the commander of space. Olson took "SPACE to be the central fact to man born in America. . . . I spell it large because it comes large here. Large, and without mercy" (CMI, 11). The problem of SPACE, unruly and resistant to our ambitions, was its conquest and hence the iconic obsession of Ahab, who embodies the triumphs of the mechanical:

> To Melville it was not the will to be free but the will to overwhelm nature that lies at the bottom of us as individuals and a people. Ahab is no democrat. Moby Dick, antagonist, is only king of natural force, resource. (CMI, 12)

To the extent that one can say that Ahab is no longer himself, it is because he is a man possessed, and "when this hell in himself yawned beneath him, a wild cry would be heard through the ship" (chapter 43, The Chart). It is not, however, as if Ahab had altogether lost his wits. His madness is focused, monomaniacal. He is coldly and impressively rational in pursuit of his irrational obsession: "all my means are sane, my motive and my object mad" (chapter 41, Moby Dick).

From whence such mad attachment? Although Ahab would be leviathan, it comes at an exorbitant cost, namely, the loss of all else that he is, and, in the destructive solipsism of obsession, the sacrifice of the Pequod. At the heart of Ahab's rational madness is the lingering inversion that Nietzsche called *ressentiment*: to see in the expanse of space my humiliation and to seek to overcome it by subjugating it to myself. Schelling in his own manner in the *Freedom* essay claimed that it was *die Angst des Lebens*, anxiety before the monstrosity of life itself, that drives us from the center and into ourselves on the periphery.[8]

Hence, when Ahab spoke to the silent severed whale head as if it were the sphinx, demanding that it speak in return, he received only monstrous silence. "O head! thou hast seen enough to split the planets and make an infidel of Abraham, and not one syllable is thine" (chapter 70, The Sphinx)! Indeed, "for unless you own the whale, you are but a provincial and sentimentalist in Truth. . . . What feel the weakling youth lifting the dread goddess's veil at Sais" (chapter 76, The Battering-Ram)? Ishmael is here alluding to what Kant in the *Critique of Judgment* deemed language's most sublime accomplishment: "Perhaps there has never been something more sublime said or a thought expressed more sublimely than that inscription over the Temple of Isis (of Mother Nature): 'I am everything that there is, that there was, and that there will be, and no mortal has lifted my veil.'"[9] Ahab is the one who becomes exclusively defined by his fixation with lifting the veil and harnessing its power for himself, seeking to dominate what the whiteness of Moby Dick evoked: "all deified nature absolutely paints like the harlot, whose allurements cover nothing but the charnel house within" (chapter 42, The Whiteness of the Whale).

Staring at his Ecuadorian coin, Ahab muses, "There's something ever egotistical in mountain-tops and towers, and all other grand and lofty things; look here,—three peaks as proud as Lucifer. The firm tower, that is Ahab; the volcano, that is Ahab; the courageous, the undaunted, and victorious fowl, that, too, is Ahab; all are Ahab" (chapter 99, The Doubloon). All that towers above the valley shall be made subject to the valley. That is how the vengeful valley seeks to live with mountains. This is confirmed as Ahab, against the lightning-filled sky, screamed, "I own thy speechless, placeless power . . . I am darkness leaping out of light, leaping out of thee" (chapter 119, The Candles).

In direct contrast with Ahab's extra-human monomania is Pip's madness, which is as wide as the vast expanses of the sea because it no longer seeks to subjugate it to his ego. "He saw God's foot upon the treadle of the loom, and spoke it; and therefore his shipmates called him mad. So man's insanity is heaven's sense; and wandering from all mortal reason, man comes at last to that celestial thought, which, to reason, is absurd and frantic" (chapter 93, The Castaway). Indeed Pip, who caws like a bird, has died to himself, and later tells the shipmen that he "died a coward" (chapter 110, Queequeg in His Coffin). Ahab at first becomes fiercely protective of Pip, sensing in him not only their shared madness, but also the vulnerability out of which madness issues. Eventually, however, Ahab must reject Pip because openness to space no longer mediated by the ego is radically incompatible with Ahab's drive to be Ahab. "Weep so, and I will murder thee! have a care, for Ahab too is mad . . . And now I quit thee" (chapter 129, The Cabin). It was all just too much, as Ahab's poignant, lonely final words to Starbuck—for what can be lonelier than a loneliness that drives one to the hermetic loneliness of solipsism?

> Forty years of continual whaling, forty years of privation, and peril, and storm time! forty years on the pitiless sea! for forty years has Ahab forsaken the peaceful land . . . —o weariness! heaviness! Guinea-coast slavery of solitary command! . . . away, whole oceans away, from that young girl-wife I wedded past fifty, and sailed for Cape Horn the next day, leaving but one dent in my marriage pillow—wife?—wife?—rather a widow with her husband alive! . . . mockery! mockery! bitter, biting mockery of grey hairs. . . . (chapter 132, The Symphony)

And so Ahab becomes trapped in the hell of being Ahab—"Ahab is for ever Ahab, man! This whole act's immutably decreed" (chapter 134, The Chase—Second Day). In dying he confirms, much as Macbeth despairs that human life is "a tale told by an idiot, full of sound and fury, signifying nothing,": "Oh, lonely death on lonely life" (chapter, 135, The Chase—Third Day).

III

Yes, this is a tragedy, but Snyder challenges us to think it not as the individual tragedy of an Ahab or a Macbeth, but rather as the tragedy of the commons.

Ishmael, always using precise details, nonetheless marvels at the final, unrepresentable monstrosity of the spermaceti whale. Given its sublimity and force, he simply can never imagine it going the way of the American bison, which, in 1851 (the year *Moby-Dick* was published), were in the process of being hunted into extinction (chapter 105, Does the Whale's Magnitude Diminish—Will He Perish?). More than a million spermaceti were likely killed during the whaling era, which ended in 1946 with the International Whaling Commission's moratorium on hunting, but the already decimated spermaceti, attempting to live in an increasingly compromised habitat, are currently listed as endangered. Snyder: "The fine information on the techniques of hand-whaling and all the steps of the flensing and rendering described in *Moby-Dick* must now, we know, be measured against the terrible specter of the extinction of whales" (PW, 127).

Ishmael's reverence for the whales, even as he hunted them, has not been widely distributed among the globalized world. It seems as if no place and no thing is sacred and if you do not want something to be taken, you have to tie it down in order to protect it from our obsessive rapacity. For Snyder, the triumph of national park systems worldwide suggests that certain places are protected for their extraordinary, even sublime qualities, but this is also to divvy things up into the pristine and the human, wilderness and urbanity, the beautiful and environmental sacrifice zones.[10] Given that we have an obsessive propensity to develop all available lands and hunt whales into extinction, we protect them from ourselves, but the result is an earth divided into them and us. This keeps us from seeing that the problem is not humans per se, but rather how contemporary industrial humans are in relationship to all other beings.

Snyder argues that other cultures have long set aside certain places not so much to sequester them from our exploitative desires as to pull us out of "our little selves" and present us not with a bifurcation of the earth into sacred and profane places, national parks and urban areas, but rather with the sacredness of the Wild. Every place is sacred. Every place matters. "Sacred refers to that which helps take us (not only human beings) out of our little selves into the whole mountains-and-rivers mandala universe" (PW, 101). It is the protection of places that teach us the value of all space and in so doing take head on *the problem of stinginess* (our lack of a serious practice of place), which prevents us from taking up the question of the Wild from the perspective of the Wild.

Who then can save Ahab from being Ahab and us from being our invasively inhabitory selves now that the great white whale is just another vulnerable ocean commodity? Snyder's answer to the problem of the new leviathan has been, for more than four decades, disarming in its simplicity: *Smokey the Bear*! In his famous sūtra of the same name, Snyder invoked a future beyond the despotism of what the Buddha diagnosed as the three poisons (greed, hatred, and delusion): "In that future American Era I shall enter a new form, to cure the world of loveless knowledge that seeks with blind hunger, and mindless rage eating food that not fill it" (PS, 25–26).

Breaking through the seemingly banal guise of Smokey the administrative bear is the once lost power of bears, and of our community with animals more broadly. This is the awakening of bears as Fudō Myō-ō (Ācala-vidyā-rāja), the Immovable Wisdom King, "patron of the Yamabushi," literally, those who take refuge in the mountains. These Shinto-Buddhist adepts still practice in the *Dewa Sanzan*, The Three Mountains of Dewa, in Yamagata Prefecture (once the ancient province of Dewa) in the relatively remote Tōhoku region of the main island of Honshu. Here the Yamabushi practitioners still endeavor to live as if they, too, were bears (PS, 29). They still undergo their severe mountain practice of *Shugendō* (and hence they are also called *Shugenja*) on these three ancient mountains (one symbolizing birth, one death, and one life), learning to awaken to the spirits (*kami*) of this place. Such living is not guided by the need to dominate, but by the compassionate power of vulnerability (PS, 30). In a sense, this is the coming of what the Buddhist tradition has sometimes called the Buddha lands, or the pure land, or the "Buddha fields [*buddha-kṣetra*]." This is not the coming of another, better place, but an awakening to a different sense of place, a sense of what is always already here as who we are. It teaches the Ahab in us all to "hark again to hear those roots, to see our ancient solidarity, and then to the work of being together on Turtle Island" (TI, introductory note).

IV

The call for an awakening to place with all of its interdependent forms of life, demands that one engage in a new humanities, beyond the Renaissance inversion of divine transcendence to anthropocentric immanence. Such an approach "would take the whole long *Homo sapiens* experience into account, and eventually make an effort to include our nonhuman kin. It would transform itself into a posthuman humanism, which would defend endangered cultures and species alike" (PS, 128). A posthuman humanities is a discourse about and for all of the creatures and all of the processes not only of Turtle Island, but the Great Earth. As we see in detail in the final chapter, it is part of an awakening to earth democracy, not just a new discipline sequestered in our increasingly expensive colleges and universities. Study is undertaken for the awakening and benefit of all. It is not just for the economically elite and it transcends what Peter Singer in *Animal Liberation* famously called speciesism.

It is also the call for the breaking through of another sense of language and therefore of other kinds of writing. Snyder's poetry often includes vernacular speech, and his prose writing is limpid and, while extraordinarily erudite, never showy. In *Turtle Island* he turns to "plain speech" and speaks of "unmuddied language and good dreams" (TI, 94). It does not take living in the Sierras to appreciate this point. Antonio Gramsci, writing from an Italian prison as the fascists consolidated their power in Italy, criticized prevailing language use as hegemonic, that is, as reflective of the implicit interests of the class elite. The unreflective dimension of common parlance is part of the illusion of the present moment: that we are indeed free and acting for ourselves when our thoughts are already coopted by ideology and, as Spinoza lamented, we fight for our slavery is if it were for our freedom. Thinking that we are fighting for ourselves, we turn against all of the creatures, human and nonhuman, that share our places and help comprise who we are. Our dreams are not even our own and are not rooted in place because we are not rooted in place.

Snyder has not only self-consciously opted to live in an intermediary or liminal place—Kitkitdizze, "in a zone of ecological recovery" (PS, 254), is on the San Juan Ridge, which is somewhat near Nevada City, but it also straddles the South and Middle Yuba rivers and abuts the Tahoe National Forest. He has also maintained an intermediary or liminal relationship with institutions. He works in them (his work on the California Arts Council under the young Governor Jerry Brown, his professorship in creative writing at UC Davis) but does not surrender himself completely to everything that they represent. Or more precisely: change comes immanently, from within the institution, but not because of or through the institution's present self-understanding. "It is not nature-as-chaos which threatens us, but the State's presumption that it has created order" (PW, 92). As we see in the concluding chapter, institutions, like our egos, are like seeds that need to split open in order to release life. This double eye and double ear also pertains to language itself. As Gramsci realized, it is already shaped by ruling interests and is not in itself automatically a language given to awakening and a Dharma revolution. "Languages were not the intellectual inventions of archaic schoolteachers, but are naturally evolved wild systems." Although it has its important and well-earned place, "good language usage," with its roots in the diction of the power elite, is rightly perceived as an essential element in the tool kit of a person hoping for success in the modern world. This last sort of writing is intrinsically boring, but it has the usefulness of a tractor that will go straight and steady up one row and down another. Like a tractor, it is expected to produce a yield: scholarly essays and dissertations, grant proposals, charges or countercharges in legalistic disputes, final reports, long-range scenarios, strategic plans. (PS, 176)

Wild writing is not about imposing one's inner life on others any more than it is about thoughtlessly reinforcing the work of Ahab's bureaucratic drones. "The more completely the world is allowed to come forward and instruct us (without the interference of ego and opinion), the better we can see our place in the interconnected world of nature" (PS, 179). This, Snyder tells us, was the practice of one of the most singular styles within the already strange and wild Zen incursions into "good language usage," namely, Dōgen Zenji, who counsels (in the *Genjō Kōan*) that "when the world of phenomena comes forth and experiences itself, it is enlightenment" (PS, 179).[11]

It is to awaken to our bioregional Buddha bear, and to care for the self as more deeply forgetting about it and awakening to our place within our bioregional place. In this light, Snyder borrows Ray Dasmann's distinction between "ecosystem cultures" and "biosphere cultures." The former make the whole of their lives and establish their ways within a "natural region, a watershed, a plant zone, a natural territory," and because this is not only the whole of their world, but the very foundation of their being, they of necessity must be "careful." "You don't destroy the soils, you don't kill all the game, you don't log it off and let the water wash the soil away" (PS, 131). Snyder has long proposed a simple practice by which we awaken and grow into our ecoculture: maintain a planetary sensibility, but dig into the place of your dwelling as if you and your gene pool would be there for many generations. Predatory inhabitation comes in, takes what it wants, and move on. "They don't care if the area becomes a wasteland. So the ecological benefit of rootedness is that people take care of a place because they realize that they're going to live there for a thousand years or more" (RW, 140–141). For his part, Snyder has inaugurated his own "Three-Hundred-Year Kitkitdizze Plan" (PS, 261).

Biosphere cultures, however, "spread their economic support system out far enough that they can afford to wreck one ecosystem and keep moving on. Well, that's Rome, that's Babylon" (PS, 131).[12] These cultures are rapaciously expansionistic, nation-states of hungry ghosts (Skt. *preta*, Jp. *gaki*), and Ahab is unable to heed the Buddha's counsel in the last moments of his life "to know how much is enough." Such consumption turns most everything into noncompostable shit, having built itself first on slavery and then on fossil fuels, and always on an expansion of itself at the expense of any serious consideration of its ecological interdependence. This is the way of taking, owning, hording, constitutive of a manner of being that requires unilateral expansionism, becoming more and more itself by becoming ever larger. They are constitutively deaf to Dōgen's claim in "*Bodaisatta Shi Shōhō* [*The Bodhisattva's Four Methods of Guidance*]" that "making a living and producing things can be nothing other than giving. To leave flowers to the wind, to leave birds to the seasons, are also acts of giving" (S, 474). What chance is there for the multigenerational patience required to develop the "capacity to hear the song of Gaia *at that spot*" when "anyone who jumps at the chance for quick profit is rewarded" (PS, 190)? This has reduced the earth, the commons that we share with all beings, to a global *tragedy of the commons*, for "any resource on earth that is not nailed down will be seen as fair game to the timber buyers or petroleum geologists from Osaka, Rotterdam, or Boston" (PW, 39).

The Buddha lands once almost broke out in the American West, even before the faint stirrings in Snyder's mid-century North Beach neighborhood (during the explosion of the San Francisco Renaissance): "Western lore has been changing from a story of exploitation and expansion by white people into a quest for a sense of place." The opening, however, was quickly shut. After Snyder's grandmother began learning to cook mushrooms and wild forest fruits in Kitsap County on the West side of Puget Sound, "the next generation grew up with supermarkets and canned food" (PS, 156).

Supermarkets allow food to appear as if from no place. They require only money or credit, but not knowledge, attentiveness, or place-based memory. In fact, powerful corporate interests often distort and obscure any knowledge about the supposed foods that are placelessly emerging in the supermarkets as if they were manna from heaven.

> How does knowledge of place help us know the Self? The answer, simply put, is that we are all composite beings, not only physically but intellectually, whose sole individual identifying feature is a particular form or structure changing constantly in time. There is no "self" to be found in that, and yet oddly enough, there is. Part of you is out there waiting to come into you, and another part of you is behind you, and the "just this" of the ever-present moment

holds all the transitory little selves in its mirror. The Avataṃsaka ("Flower Wreath") jeweled-net-interpenetration-ecological systems-emptiness-consciousness tells us no self-realization without the Whole Self, and the whole self is the whole thing. (PS, 189)

Ethics, therefore, is not first and foremost an issue of individual responsibility. Ethics is rather the demand that we think *more fully as place*. "Whatever sense of ethical responsibility and concern that human beings can muster must be translated from a human-centered consciousness to a natural-systems-wide sense of value" (PS, 210) rather than reducing the nonhuman forces of our bioregions to "primarily a building-supply yard for human projects" (PS, 237). Indeed, we are at a clear and precarious crossroad: either "we make a world-scale 'Natural Contract' with the oceans, the air, the birds in the sky" (PW, 39) or we succumb to madness at heart of the tragedy of the commons—the decimation of the earth itself as the byproduct of our self-striving.

Although I return to the prospects for a Natural Contract in the concluding chapter, for now we can note that there is also a hint of something anarchic about it. In contrast with common parlance, anarchy, just like the Wild, does not mean chaos and the triumph of the arbitrary. The Wild at its heart is sovereign, freely unfolding within itself as necessity. The Dharma is spontaneous, but that speaks to the emptiness of each place, an emptiness discernable only through increased attentiveness to the concrete particulars of that place. The Wild is anarchic, but orderly, while the State is orderly but only superficially so; its sense of order is not attentive to the place that comprises it. In a sense, the State is the delusion that we can continue to order place to accord with our interests. As "The Surre(gion)alist Manifesto" poses the choice between the anarchy of the Wild and the anthropocentric order of the State: "The Region is against the Regime" (quoted in PW, 48). In the long run, "the United States, Canada, Mexico, are passing political entities" (PW, 44). This is not to deny their own manner of legitimacy and it is not to abandon all hope that these nations can come to understand themselves differently.[13] Historically, however, "civilization itself is ego gone to seed and institutionalized in the form of the State, both Eastern and Western" (PW, 99–100).

But just as the clouds move across the earth, unconcerned about political alliances, the Way knows no discernible first principle, no comprehensible *archē* (ἀρχή), which governs and controls the Wild. The Wild requires a "full and sensitive acknowledgement of the subjecthood—and intrinsic value—of nature" (PS, 246). The lack of a discernible *archē*, however, means not only that the Wild is not originally any *one* thing, but that it is also not vaguely and mysteriously *all one*. The Great Earth is a great Indra's net of interrelated bioregional systems and hence "bioregionalism calls for commitment" to Turtle Island "*place by place*, in terms of biogeographical regions and watersheds" (PS, 246). "To know the spirit of a place is to realize that you are a part of a part and that the whole is made of parts, each of which is whole. You start with the part you are whole in" (PW, 41). The practice of the Wild begins with who we are, which is *how we practice where we are right now*: how we eat, how we otherwise consume, how we build, how we teach, how we write, how we speak to each other, how we make politics, how we plant gardens.

The dominant biosphere cultures, including our own, are challenged to acknowledge that they are possessed by the hungry ghosts that ruled Ahab, but they are also invited to be what Snyder called *re-inhabitory*, that is, "to become people who are learning to live and think 'as if' they were totally engaged with their place for the long future" (PS, 247). We are called to wake up to ourselves, to undergo Pope Francis' "ecological conversion," to be *born again* (PW, 43), and to become part of a "worldwide purification of mind" (PW, 44), that is, to become inhabitants of *where we are as what we are*: re-inhabitants of Turtle Island, where a "vast past, an open future, and all the life communities of plants, humans, and critters come into focus" (PS, 248).

4

Bears
(The Many Palaces of the Earth)

I don't invent things out of my head unless it is an actual experience—
like seeing a bear in a dream, this is a true mode of seeing a bear.
—Gary Snyder (RW, 20)

I

In *Mountains and Rivers Without End*, after Tārā has exposed the great communion of all beings ("An Offering for Tārā"), the bear mother finally appears and she did not wear a ranger's hat and blue jeans like Smokey the Bear:

> She veils herself
> >   to speak of eating salmon
> >   Teases me with
> >   "What do you know of my ways"
> >   And kisses me through the mountain.
>
> Through and under its layers, its
> >   gullies, its folds;
> >   Her mouth full of blueberries.
> >   We share. (MR, 115)

Like the Yamabushi, we encounter the spirits (*kami*) of the mountains, who tell us that we do not know their ways. The human relationship to the bear who insists on her own ways—not the ways of an anthropomorphized Smokey the Bear—is among the oldest tropes in Snyder's poetry. In "A Berry Feast," performed at the legendary Six Gallery poetry reading on Friday, October 7, 1955, which launched the San Francisco Renaissance, we are also introduced to the bear through its redolent scat:

> Bear has been eating the berries.
>> high meadow, late summer, snow gone
> Blackbear
>> eating berries, married
> To a woman whose breasts bleed
> From nursing the half-human cubs. (BC, 13)

What manner of marriage is this? How does a woman relate to a bear, indeed, give birth to and nurse their half-human cubs? These questions—and variations of the myth about the woman who married this berry loving bear—are scattered widely among indigenous peoples of the north. Who is this bear lurking within the facade of Smokey and how and where do we meet it?

II

This encounter with the bear begins with the realization that our relationship with bears has taken an unprecedented turn for the worst. In the coterminus United States and Mexico, brown bears—*ursus arctos* (the bear of all bears, from first the Latin and then the Greek words for bear)—have yielded 99 percent of their former range to human encroachment and anthropocentric land management.[1] Although they have no known predators except for humans, the latter have proven themselves to be devastatingly formidable at predation. In 1975, the *ursus arctos horribilis* (the grizzly bear) was listed as threatened in the lower states, having dropped from an estimated 50,000 bears in 1800 to less than a thousand and today it shows faint signs of recovery, although its range has been reduced to the Yellowstone National Park ecosystem as well as to the northern continental divide, including Glacier National Park, both of whose populations now exceed five hundred each. Miniscule scatterings of grizzly can be found in Washington and Idaho (the Selkirks, North Cascades National Park, and the Cabinet-Yaak ecosystem, which also extends into western Montana). The enormous *ursus arctos californicus* was driven into extinction in the 1920s, although it survives on the California state flag as well as a sports mascot (the UC Berkeley Golden Bears and the UCLA Bruins, an old term for brown bears derived from the Dutch word for brown). The Mexican grizzly bear (the *ursus arctos nelsoni*, but known locally as *el oso plateado*, the silver bear) has not been seen since the early 1960s and is presumed extinct. The *ursus arctos ugavaesis*, once found on the quite remote Ungava Peninsula in far northern Quebec, was hunted to extinction by 1913. Times of ancient truces and cohabitation between first nations peoples and bears are over and Snyder tells us that "the bears are being killed, the humans are everywhere, and the green world is being unraveled and shredded and burned by the spreading of a gray world that seems to have no end" (PW, 181).

The graying of the world has not only resulted in the current climate emergency—the Intergovernmental Panel on Climate Change's Fifth Assessment Report confirms that "total anthropogenic GHG [greenhouse gas] emissions were the highest in human history from 2000 to 2010."[2] The situation has continued its dramatic decline since then with each year breaking the record of the year before—nothing like a climate emergency to spur human action! The pledge by 176 countries and the EU in the Paris Agreement (*L'accord de Paris*), sealed in December 2015 and signed in April 2016 (beginning on Earth Day), to restrict global warming "well below 2 degrees Celsius [3.6 degrees Fahrenheit]," even if met, is likely to be too little too late. While clearly better than nothing, the actions pledged in the agreement, even if they are actualized, are not enough to meet a goal that in itself is too modest. A 2 degree Celsius change is likely still large enough to continue to precipitate the tumultuous transition to a different kind of earth. We are also amid the Sixth Extinction event with the greatest rate of species loss since the collapse of the great reptiles[3] as well as the greatest explosion of human births in the earth's history (it increased by 700 percent in the past two centuries). We seem hell-bent on becoming too gray for the brown bear.

Schopenhauer once lamented that "Christian morals has no regard for animals, so in philosophical morals, these are immediately fair game, just 'things,' just *means* to favored ends, thus something for vivisection, coursing, bullfighting, horse-racing, and whipping to death before an immovable stone cart, etc."[4] Even Kant (or Levinas after him) could not wrench himself from this prejudice, arguing that moral duty extends to animals only insofar as it is an extension of our duty to ourselves. Kant stingily argued that we should resist cruelty to animals only because it inculcates bad habits and weakens our "relations *to other humans*," leading Schopenhauer to quip that "thus one should have compassion with animals just for practice, and animals are, as it were, the pathological phantom for the practice of compassion toward humans" (BM, 172–173). (Variations of this kind of argument were sometimes also used to justify a more merciful treatment of slaves.)

Indeed, subspecies of *ursus arctos* were once widespread throughout Eurasia and North Africa, although they are now generally only found in remote areas like Siberia, islands like Hokkaido and Sakhalin, and the Himalayas, where the critically endangered Himalayan brown bear (*ursus arctos isabellinus*)—rumored to have been the source of the legends of the Yeti—has been reduced to a few hundred survivors and is already extinct in Bhutan. The Atlas Bear, which ranged in the mountains of North Africa, was hunted to extinction before the turn of the nineteenth century; in Italy, likely less than forty Marsican (or Apennine) brown bears survive within the Abruzzo National Park and vicinity.

In his 1924 dissertation (published in 1926), the University of Pennsylvania anthropologist Alfred Irving Hallowell argued for the remarkable "intercontinental analogies" of bear ceremonies among diverse indigenous peoples that were as widespread as the worldwide historical range of bears.[5] Regardless of how one comes down on the issue of continuity among these ceremonies, the evidence suggests that they were both ancient and prevalent among most all of the lands shared by humans and bears. The evidence is overwhelming that our species once had a very different relationship with bears. More recently, Michel Pastoureau, in his revelatory historical study, *The Bear: History of a Fallen King*, tells us that in Saxony and nearby areas, until the rise of Charlemagne and the early German Catholic Church, "the bear was sometimes venerated as a god, which gave rise to forms of worship that were sometimes frenetic or demonic, particularly among warriors. Bears had to be absolutely eradicated to convert these barbarians to the religion of Christ. It was a difficult, almost impossible task, because these cults were neither recent nor superficial."[6]

In the late work *Götzen-Dämmerung* (1888), Nietzsche railed against moral "improvement [*Verbesserung*]" by way of the "domestication of the beast-human [*Zähmung der Bestie Mensch*]"[7]—breeding by way of the sickening and slackening of the humanimal (another way of saying *Bestie Mensch*). One domesticates by using pain to make the beast weaker, more decadent, scattered, and divided. "Whoever knows what takes place in a menagerie doubts that the beast is being 'improved' by it. . . . In the early Middle Ages, where in fact the church was first and foremost a menagerie, the most beautiful exemplars of the 'blond beast' were hunted down everywhere—one 'improved,' for example, the noble and salubrious [*vernehm*] Germans" (KSA 6: 99). The disappearance of the brown bear in most all of Europe was already so much so a fact that for Nietzsche the image of these "blonde beasts of prey" evoked lions,[8] but we now know from Pastoureau that these noble barbarians were not really lions—lions came to Europe thanks to zoos and circuses. They were rather those who understood themselves in relationship to the divinity of bears. The brown bear that roamed the countryside and forests of Christian Europe into the High Middles Ages was "larger and wilder than the bear that still inhabits in small numbers a few wooded mountains on the old continent. The medieval bear had a more carnivorous diet than today's brown bear; it was taller and heavier, its coat was darker, its fur stiffer, and its claws sharper. That bear shared with the Devil, or at least with the image retained of the Devil, several physical attributes that facilitated Satan's disguise as a bear . . . " (BH, 128).

I would add that the canonical image of the devil—half goat and half person—also evokes the figure of the pagan Dionysus. The brown bear was deposed as the Dionysian god of the north. "The long war that the Church had been fighting against the bear since the Merovingian period really began to bear fruit after the year 1000. Physically eliminated by systematic hunts, symbolically vanquished by a large number of saints, demonized by texts, images, and sermons, in the High Middles Ages the bear finally descended from his throne and joined the parade of ordinary animals" (BH, 135). As Europe civilized itself, as it took possession of what belonged to it by right, as it took rightful possession of its land, the labor that entitled us to call the land our own consisted most of all of the difficult and enduring work of managerially *improving* the land. Snyder: "It is hard to even begin to gauge how much a complication of possessions, the notions of 'my and mine,' stand between us and a true, clear, liberated way of seeing the world" (TI, 98–99).

How did one ever come into contact with the bear, not as a big and threatening mammal, but as the indicator species of a spiritual ecology? We take our first clue from William Faulkner's justly celebrated novella, "The Bear," from the interrelated narratives that comprise *Go Down, Moses* (1942),[9] which, when taken as a whole, can also be read as a novel in which the possessed and enslaved (human and nonhuman) are likened to the Israelites in their quest for liberation. To the young Ike McCaslin, the bear dwelled in the fast disappearing dreamtime realm of the forest: "it loomed and towered in his dreams before he even saw the unaxed woods where it left its crooked print, shaggy, tremendous, red-eyed, not malevolent but just big . . . too big for the very country that was its constricting scope . . . it was as if the boy had already divined . . . that doomed wilderness whose edges were being constantly and punily gnawed at by men with plows and axes who feared it because it was wilderness" (B, 141).

Where does one travel to meet the aged god, Old Ben, who dwells, as shamans know, in the dreamtime realm? My entire reflection rests on the answer to this question. For Faulkner, one could not meet the ancient bear god on the default ground of one's humanity, as ancient shamans have also contended (evidenced, for example, in cave paintings and petroglyphs found all over the earth), but rather only by entering the time and space in which the worlds (and life forms) of human and bear touch upon one other. Ike divined encountering the bear "shadowy in the limbo from which time emerged and became time: the old bear absolved of mortality and himself who shared a little of it" (B, 149).

A very young Ike, eleven years old, vainly sets off with his new Christmas gift, a breech-loader, to find Old Ben. Sam Fathers, the "son of negro slave and a Chickasaw chief" (B, 151), tells Ike that he would have to choose between the gun and the bear and so the next morning Ike, driven by his desire to see the bear, sets out only with a compass and a "stick for snakes," abrogating not only the conditions of Old Ben's "heretofore inviolable anonymity" but also the ancient rules that governed hunter and hunted (B, 152). He then discards another attachment: his fear of the bear. Soon he realized that even this was not enough if he wanted to relinquish himself completely to the "markless wilderness." Yes, "he was still tainted," and so he removed his watch and compass, abdicating the anthropocentric management of time and space. He was entering the time-space of limbo, remembering all that Sam had taught him. "Then he saw the bear. It did not emerge, appear" (B, 153). The bear caught sight of Ike over one of its shoulders and then disappeared as if it were a fish tracelessly submerging into the dark depths of the water (B, 153–154).

Eventually the annual November whiskey drinking and hunting party sports a fearless dog, Lion, who eventually tracks Old Ben, and ferociously digs its teeth into his throat while the bear defensively clawed at the dog's abdomen, allowing Boon Hogganbeck to come at it from behind with his knife, "working and probing the buried blade" (B, 177). The bear stood up again, lurched two or three steps forward, and then "fell all of a piece, as a tree falls" (B, 178). Like the forest under the axe, Old Ben fell to the earth. Lion died of his wounds and Sam Fathers collapsed and soon died thereafter.

At this point, three more observations offer themselves.

1. The historic range of the brown bear never extended to Mississippi, but two species of black bear have survived: the *ursus americanus*

or common back bear, whose habitat is found in the more northerly parts of the state, but which is currently listed as endangered in that state, and in southern Mississippi the much rarer Louisiana black bear (*ursus americanus luteolus*), federally listed as threatened.
2. Old Ben—the old god—is deposed by a dog called Lion, who, for all is vestigial wildness, was also a more docile companion. Pastoureau tells us that the long war on the bear, "a long term phenomenon, the apex of which was undoubtedly the twelfth century, at least in Western Europe" (BH, 152), finally came to an end as the bear abdicated its throne to the lion. The latter were now "encountered everywhere . . . painted, carved, modeled, embroidered, woven, described, recounted, thought about, and dreamed" (BH, 136). The bear's journey to the docile teddy bear was underway as lions are brought in and trained to be the figurehead deities of a new kind of world, ferocious (on our terms), but overseeing the destruction of a different sense of time and space.
3. Snyder observes that "bears are the closest of all animals to humans. Everybody says, 'After you take a bear's coat off, it looks just like a human.' And they act human: they fool, they teach their cubs (who are rowdy and curious), and they remember. . . . Their claws are delicate and precise: they can pick up a nut between two tips. They make love for hours. They are grumpy after naps" (PW, 175). Alas, we entered a period in which there seemed to be room for only one world on the earth.

A few years after the death of Old Ben, after Ike had turned twenty-one, it came time to inherit "the tamed land which was to have been his heritage" (B, 188), but he repudiated it precisely because "it was never mine to repudiate" and the "men who bought it bought nothing" (B, 189). His grandfather, old Carothers McCaslin, had "got the land no matter how" (B, 189) and endeavored to tame it by appropriating the forced labor of his slaves, "the beings he held in bondage and in power of life and death" (B, 188), who consequently deforested the land in order to cultivate crops.

In the fifth chapter of the *Second Treatise of Civil Government*, John Locke influentially argued that "though the earth, and all inferior creatures, be common to all men,"—humans already own the bears, albeit in common—"every man has a property in his own person: this no body has any right to but himself." Human beings first and foremost own themselves; we are our own private property. Locke nonetheless thought there could be legitimate forms of slavery (the appropriation of the enemy in a just war, hardly an apt description of the Trans-Atlantic Slave Trade).[10] Moreover, he was both personally invested in the slave trade through his lucrative holdings in the Royal African Company and an author of *Fundamental Constitutions of Carolina* (adopted March 1, 1669), whose 110th article proclaimed that "Every Freeman of Carolina shall have absolute power and Authority over his Negro slaves, of what opinion or Religion soever" and this "absolute power and Authority" included the right to murder one's slave with impunity.[11] One could dispose with one's property in any way that one saw fit.

Ultimately, how do we come to own the earth and its creatures that Genesis declares we hold in common? "The labor of his body, and the work of his hands," Locke argues, "are properly his. Whatsoever then he removes out of the state that nature hath provided, and left it in, he hath mixed his labor with, and joined to it something that is his own, and thereby makes it his property" (section 27). When I labor for years in the woods to shoot the bear, the pelt is mine. I have rightfully appropriated it, so long as I do not take so much that I hinder others from their own appropriative efforts.

Ike retorted by insisting that the God of *Genesis* clearly had not given anyone the earth "to hold for himself and his descendants inviolable title forever, generation after generation" but rather to "to hold the earth mutual and intact in the communal anonymity of brotherhood" (B, 190). Was not the dispossession of Eden already an indication that the earth was not ours? Did not reading Scriptures with one's heart confirm this? This certainly did not include the right to own others as property, to appropriate them as chattel, not to mention the great crimes (rape, incest, Eunice's suicide by drowning as a consequence of such crimes, etc.) that Carothers McCaslin committed as he disposed of his property as he saw fit. If slavery is the most conspicuous karmic scar on Mississippi, it is related to its root in the destruction of the land by appropriation.

As Schopenhauer also recognized in his refreshingly iconoclastic fashion, the Bible would not have been much help with respect to slavery. "Whoever wants to deny compassion [*Mitleid*] as the incentive for this fine, large scale action in order to ascribe it to Christianity, should recall that in the whole New Testament not one word is said against slavery" (BM, 232). In both Testaments there are numerous passages that take ancient forms of slavery (in which slaves did not possess their selves, offspring, labor, or sexual autonomy) as a fact of life, even when, for example, Saint Paul sends the slave Onesimus back to Philemon, beseeching Philemon to treat him as a dear brother, a "brother in the Lord," welcoming "Onesimus as you would welcome me" (Philemon I: 16–18, NIRV). This might be improvement for Onesimus, and abolitionists had vainly attempted to enlist this passage on behalf of their cause, but Paul does not make his plea a part of an unequivocal ethical rejection of the institution of owning slaves as such.

To be fair, slavery does not originate in the Bible, which merely acknowledges it as a fact of human life and occasionally seeks to ameliorate it. With or without it, owning humans, oversight of the earth and suzerainty over the animals (per Genesis) (B, 190), and the destruction of forests and other ancient ecosystems for plantations, estates, and other starkly anthropocentric zones, all expressed the same type of unrelenting disposition. In slavery, we treat humans as we treat animals, all of which are part and parcel of how we assume that the Great Earth is at our disposal. As such, we could not be farther away from Dōgen in "*Kūge* [*Flowers in the Sky/Flowers of Emptiness*]" when he, following Song Dynasty Caodong Master SHIMEN Huiche, proclaims that "flowers in the sky emerge from the entire earth, open blossoms, emerging from the entire earth." While both the flowers and the flowering itself of emptiness "emerge from the earth," "the whole nation has no way to buy them," that is, "it is not that the whole nation does not buy them; it is just that there is no way to buy them" (S, 467).

Finally, when Ike returned to the camp and saw Boon "one more time before the lumber company moved in and began to cut the lumber" (B, 234), he found him sitting against the trunk of a tree, which "seemed to be alive with frantic squirrels. There appeared to be forty or fifty of them leaping and darting from branch to branch" (B, 245). Old Boon was desperately trying to rebuild his gun "with the frantic abandon of a madman," hammering the breech, screaming, "Get out of here! Don't touch them! Don't touch a one of them! They're mine" (B, 246)! Animals belong to us, although in the accursed land of Faulkner's Mississippi, as the celebrated Martinican literary critic Edouard Glissant, whose own ancestors were enslaved, reflects, "property is seen as the death of the natural order. Ultimately, this is a condemnation, if not of the peopling of the land, at least of the original methods and future consequences of this occupation." Glissant distances Faulkner from the naïveté of someone like Rousseau or Proudhon, speaking rather of Faulkner's "affirmation of a pantheist reality (the invigorating solidarity among nature's species) outside of which all other human, social, political, or economic demands lose their meaning. There is a remarkable obsolescence in these words that leads, however, in a most pertinent way, to what threatens us today."[12]

III

Faulkner's narrative, however, is a narrative told from the dawning guilt consciousness of the vast enterprise of appropriation. Ike repudiates his own forsaken and accursed ancestry, although the memory of Old Ben, like Sam Fathers, also has the remoteness of the dreams in which Old Ben and his Dharma practice realm first appeared. These are stories of what once was, but they are facilitated by the cultures whose conditions of possibility also condemn to the past the very things their artists and historians later recount. Even Pastoureau's remarkable history depends on a culture in which the divinity of bears, which always were where the wild things are and which remain most present to children before they have been improved into adults, has been re-engineered into an endless consumer market for teddy bears. Pastoureau: "In the twentieth century, zoo and circus bears were no longer the only types of bear that amused children. The animal gradually entered every house, every bedroom, in the form of a toy, and was becoming the child's closest companion" (BK, 247).

How would "The Bear" have been told from the perspective of Sam Fathers? Or if we tried, as demanding and limited as such a vision would be, to approach the perspective of the bears themselves? What narratives would have been told if Pastoureau lived in a world in which his calling was not to preside over the funeral of the bear gods? Snyder recalls a story, first hinted at, as we have seen, in his breakthrough 1955 poem "A Berry Feast," that comes to us because of the intervention of anthropology, that study of the great forest of the human condition, albeit mostly from the perspective of the plantation. (Snyder's remarkable style of anthropology is emblematic of a different approach to this discipline.) "The Woman Who Married a Bear" was recounted by Maria Johns of the Tlingit and Athabascan speaking peoples of southern Yukon Territory to the anthropologist Catherine McClellan in 1948 and it appeared in 1970 in the latter's *The Girl Who Married the Bear: A Masterpiece of Indian Oral Tradition*, which analyzes eleven variations of this extraordinary narrative.[13]

Snyder's version of the shamanic middle world, the encounter "shadowy in the limbo from which time emerged and became time," in which woman and bear meet, combines the shamanic with the remarkable Zen writing and practice of Dōgen. "There's a world behind the world that we see that is the same world but more open, more transparent, without blocks. Like inside a big mind, the animals and humans all can talk, and those who pass through here get power to heal and help.... To touch this world no matter however briefly is a help in life. People seek it, but the seeking isn't easy. Shapes are fluid here. For a bear, all the beings look like bears. For a human, they all look like humans" (PW, 176).

To cross this "borderline," Snyder evokes a remarkable passage from the *Sansui-kyō*, which, in turn, evokes a remarkable passage from Dōgen's *Genjō Kōan*. In the former, Dōgen tells us that "hungry ghosts see water as raging fire or pus and blood. Dragons and fish see water as a palace or pavilion," that is, "water is seen as dead or alive depending on [the seer's] causes and conditions" (S, 159). In *Genjō Kōan* we are told that the practice of the fish demands water—"if the fish leaves the water, it will die at once" (S, 32)—while the practice of the bird requires the air. Each must find its element, each must find the *place where its practice occurs*. This is *Genjō Kōan*, actualizing the fundamental point: finding the place where your practice occurs. This means, however, that we must see the water and air as practice, that the emptiness of water and air must somehow become present in their emptiness as constitutive of presentation as such. Moreover, while these elements are multiple, they are not separable, but belong to the immense variegation of the Buddha sea. "Shapes are fluid here. For a bear, all the beings look like bears. For a human, they all look like humans" (PW, 176).

These considerations help contextualize the passage from *Sansui-kyō* that Snyder deploys to help articulate the in-between, the *marriage* between a woman and a bear:

> When dragons and fish see water as a palace, it may be like human beings seeing a palace. They may not think it flows. If an outsider tells them, "What you see as a palace is running water," the dragons and fish may be astonished, just as we are when we hear the words *Mountains flow*. (S, 161; see PW, 176)

When the in-between, the flowing emptiness that is the insubstantiality of all beings, suddenly presents itself in its luminous darkness, it is indeed astonishing. As David Foster Wallace famously elaborated in his 2005 Commencement Address at Kenyon College:

> There are these two young fish swimming along and they happen to meet an older fish swimming the other way, who nods at them and says "Morning, boys. How's the water?" And the two young fish

swim on for a bit, and then eventually one of them looks over at the other and goes "What the hell is water?"[14]

Water is the palace of a fish, but it is not the palace of a human. (For this reason, we are right to shun the absurd aspiration that we will go to Mars to escape the devastation that we have wrought on earth.) Bears and humans have shared the palace of the mountains, although, as the rigors of the Yamabushi practice of *Shugendō* demonstrate, sharing is rarely easy. The Great Earth is comprised of myriad intersecting palaces. All creatures would find it astonishing that they live in palaces. Humans for their part are astonished to learn that palaces are not the *things* that they are used to calling places (mountains, valleys, islands, peninsulas, deserts, forests, farmlands, towns, cities). The walking or flowing of mountains, the wilding of the town and the city, the emptiness and interdependent vitality of bioregions, is also what is astonishing to learn about regarding our own palaces. It is astonishing to learn that our place is a palace, not just resources at our disposal.

It is also remarkable that in most all of the variations of the story, it is a woman who enters the flowing water of the in-between. Pastoureau recounts that many European bear stories also "held that bears were fond of girls and young women. A bear would sometimes be a lover or a seducer, more often an abductor and rapist; he would seize them and carry them off to his den where he would have monstrous sexual relations with them, which sometimes resulted in half-human, half-bear offspring" (BK, 72).

Of course, this reflects the immense anxiety of the property obsessed patriarchy, but it is also astonishing that William of Auvergne (c. 1180 or 1190–1249), who made his name protecting the Christian faith from the new Latin translations of the Greek (Aristotelian), Islamic, and Jewish traditions, despite his admiration for some of their philosophical accomplishments, and who contributed to a papal bull that culminated in the ransacking of Jewish libraries and the eventual burning of their books, nonetheless acknowledged that the bear is the closest animal to the human. He also maintained that the bear had human enough sperm so that its offspring with women were not *monstri* but rather *veri homines*, fully human (BK, 78). Women, for the patriarchs, are a minimally human part of humanity, and bears, the least animal part of animality. They could, at least until the triumph of the lions, produce true bear-humans.

In the story, the bear initially appeared human and the woman and the bear feasted on berries and gopher meat. Until the autumn, when it came time to dig the den, the woman never figured out that he was a bear. Except when he was digging, he always looked like a human. The woman, not to be tracked by her three brothers and their dogs, rubbed sand over her body and vicinity (PW, 168). At first, time was slow: "every time they camped it seemed like a month to her, but it really was only a day" (PW, 167); but soon time began to flow and "each month" in the cave "seemed like another morning" (PW, 169). In the middle of the winter, she had two babies with her ursine husband. When it came time for the brown bear to emerge for the spring, his wife begged him not to kill his brothers-in-law, who would come hunting for bear meat. "Just think of the kids. Don't hurt my brothers" (PW, 170)!

Her husband departed for the last time and was soon slaughtered by the brothers. In accordance with her husband's final wishes, the mournful wife burned his head and tail, and sang his shamanic songs (akin to the kind of bear ceremonies that Hallowell described). She returned to the village with her two children, but she could not yet live with her old family—"she wasn't used to the human smell" (PW, 172)—and so she lived in a nearby encampment. The following spring, her brothers taunted her, goading her to wear the pelt of a female bear that they had just killed. "I can't do it! Once I do it, I will turn into a bear. I'm half there already" (PW, 172). Nonetheless, her brothers persevered, and when they stealthily covered her with the bear pelt, she became a grizzly and killed her two oldest brothers as well as her mother in self-defense. Only the youngest brother—the animal furthest from the transformation into human adulthood—survived. The bear returned to the mountains with her children.

Maria Johns concluded that this revealed the proximity of humans to *ursus arctos horribilis* and for that reason "they still don't eat Grizzly meat, because Grizzlies are half human" (PW, 172). In a much different time and space where bears were systematically dethroned, William of Auvergne could still assert that bear flesh tasted like human flesh—How did he know?—and that the human consumption of bear meat and the ursine consumption of human flesh amounted to cannibalism (BK, 78).

"We are always in both worlds," Snyder argues, "because they aren't really two" (PW, 177). Bears long ago learned to share berries and salmon with humans—one need only think of the bemused expression of the bears as Timothy Treadwell, who hated civilization, "protected" them in Werner Herzog's classic *Grizzly Man* (2005) or the fact that an older itinerant bear eventually consumed him and his girlfriend. From the perspective of the Great Earth, its myriad palaces are not myriad. From the perspective of bears, it is hard to appreciate the human palace. From the perspective of humans, it is hard, as the woman who married a bear and Ike McCaslin both learned, to put one's own palace into enough relief that one can enter the palace of a bear. "One cannot cross between realms without paying a high price" (PW, 181) Snyder warns. The woman and her husband "live at timberline" (PW, 177), but her brothers could not "stand this ambiguity" (PW, 180) and each palace was left ruinously to its own.

Gary Snyder has referred to his study of this story as "depth ecology," that is, "a territory where myth or folklore or shamanic constructions have to do with the way you treat creatures, whether or not you kill them or don't kill them. How do you kill a bear" (NH, 37)? These myths and stories belong to the ecologies of particular places—the external landscape of the place and the internal landscape of its creatures. They are the *upāya* by which we learn better to enter the depths of our internal and external landscapes and at the same time they teach us that the Great Earth is Tārā and her endless arms of compassion, each one a palace.

PART III

Earth Democracy

◆ 5 ◆

The Great Potlatch

> . . . For the
> *puja*, the ritual, the offering, the meal,
>
> Marpa purifying Milarepa,
> "Build it again!" Snapping
> snap-lines, setting levels, placing stones. (MR, 110)

I

The concluding section of this book turns to a philosophic and poetic inquiry into the prospects in the thought of Snyder for earth democracy. This chapter begins this inquiry somewhat indirectly by considering the ritual gift-giving feast called potlatch as an image, both archaic and radically futural, of how to *re-inhabit* the Great Earth. But does one not just study potlatch by reading books and going to anthropological museums? Or even more to the point: How could any of this make sense of re-inhabitation? What is re-inhabitation and why should we strive to re-inhabit a place that we already putatively inhabit?

In an "Offering for Tārā," we are brought to the dynamically interlocking movement of giving and taking—"a puja, a potluck / for the whole Himalayan plateau" (MR, 113). Potluck in common parlance can sound like the rather stingy dinner invitation where everyone has to bring their own food but Snyder tells us that the potluck does not have to be understood like this; his late wife Carole Koda recalled that the potluck was the basic practice of the Jōdo Shinshū community of her youth.[1] The "other power (*ta-riki*)" of the True Pure Land sect, as opposed the "self-power (*ji-riki*)" emphasis of practices like Zen, was centered in this case on a meal that helped one get beyond oneself. Our typical attitude toward food and consumption obscures the fact that in the communion of all beings, we are *both* eaters and the eaten. "All of biological nature can be seen as an enormous *puja*, a ceremony of offering and sharing" (PS, 77).

In our ego-reinforcing inhabitory mind-sets, however, we see ourselves lopsidedly as consumers. The weak are meat and the strong need to eat! The Great Earth, however, is the full range of communion, not just the self-serving portion. For this reason, Tārā always takes the side of those without power, of those that Pope Francis called the "abandoned and maltreated of our poor" (LS, 3), including, for both Tārā and Francis, the Great Earth herself. Hence: "Tārā's vow / 'Those who wish to attain supreme enlightenment / in a man's body are many . . . / therefore may I, / *until this world is emptied out*, / serve the needs of beings / with my body of a woman'" (MR, 110–111). It is not that the Earth or Nature is more female than male or that in the end it even makes much sense to assign it a gender. It is that Tārā, on behalf of earth democracy, takes the side of the more vulnerable. She extends her constituency to represent the least obvious and most noticed parts of earth democracy. Communion begins when we hear the geological voice of Tārā and Gaia. "To hear her voice is to give up the European word 'America' and accept the new-old name for the continent, 'Turtle Island'" (TI, 105).

It is my contention in this chapter that Tārā's gift—"leading-water, / moving stones" (MR, 114)—in its ritual reenactments, which includes the Sōtō Zen chant before and after taking a meal, especially the lines "Now we set out Buddha's own bowls / May we, with all living beings / realize the emptiness of the three wheels, / giver, receiver, and gift," celebrates an awakening that enables us to *appreciate* that we generally dwell poorly in our dwellings, that we inhabit places without appreciating either habitation or place. This dawning appreciation is a transformative wake-up call, demanding that we begin to experiment with what Snyder called the "re-inhabitatory," which "refers to the tiny number of persons who come out of the industrial societies (having collected or squandered the fruits of 8000 years of civilization) and then start to turn back to the land, to place. This comes for some with the rational and scientific realization of interconnectedness, and planetary limits. But the actual demands of a life committed to a place, and living somewhat by the sunshine green plant energy that is concentrating in that spot, are so physically and intellectually intense, that it is a moral and spiritual choice as well."[2]

It is to enter intentionally the Big Potlatch and its rituals, old and new, as the possibility of dwelling wakefully in our respective places on and as the Great Earth. Of course, such words sound foolish and eccentric these days with the continued rise of consumerism and self-aggrandizement. But such a maleficent image is the image of a place where potlatch membership entails no acknowledgment of the potlatch (offering the place to itself) and consequently no responsibility to it and gratitude for it.

II

In his famous 1809 essay on *Human Freedom*, Schelling characterized our current alienation from nature as constitutive of the modern period, which has, "since its inception (in Descartes) the shared deficiency that nature is not present to it and that it lacks Nature's living ground."[3] It was not that we had discovered science and therefore found nature for the first time, but rather that our matter of doing science separated science not only from the realm of human affairs, but also from the Wild itself.

In a more contemporary idiom, Bruno Latour has criticized the modern diremption of Being into the political and the natural, the former characterized by the political science of Hobbes and the latter characterized by Boyle's conception of the scientific realm (or natural world), which inaugurates "a political discourse from which politics is to be excluded."[4] The politics that valorize what counts as science are eventually banished from the practice of science, while the "science" that supposedly anchors political science yields no meaningful experiments. Science studies the artificial realm that we imagine is the detached, apolitical, and objective natural world; political and social life operates in an opposed subjective realm. This Modern Constitution cleanly cleaves the social and the natural, the political and the organic, nurture and nature, allowing all manner of hybrids to abound and haunt the interstices of this great modern divide. Traditional culture-natures soon came under the wilting force of this great schism.

> Native Americans were not mistaken when they accused the Whites of having forked tongues. By separating the relations of political power from the relations of scientific reasoning while continuing to shore up power with reason and reason with power, the moderns have always had two irons in the fire. They have become invincible.
>
> You think that thunder is a divinity? The modern critique will show you that it is generated by mere physical mechanisms that have no influence over the progress of human affairs. You are stuck in a traditional economy? The modern critique will show you that

> physical mechanisms can upset the progress of human affairs by mobilizing huge productive forces. . . . You think that you can do everything and develop your societies as you see fit? The modern critique will show you that the iron laws of society are much more inflexible than those of your ancestors. (WNM, 38)

Before the power of the Modern, everything else is premodern, primitive, archaic, quaint, mere anthropological curiosities and exotica.

Snyder has also discerned this strange fork in the emergence of a strange species of "city-dweller" called the Modern Philosopher (Snyder cites Descartes, Newton, and Hobbes) who found a way to banish the nonhuman world.

> These thinkers were as hysterical about "chaos" as their predecessors, the witch-hunt prosecutors of only a century before, were about "witches." They not only didn't enjoy the possibility that the world is as sharp as the edge of a knife, they wanted to take that edge away from nature. Instead of making the world safer for humankind, the foolish tinkering with the powers of life and death by the occidental scientist-engineer-ruler puts the whole planet on the brink of degradation. Most of humanity—foragers, peasants, or artisans—has always taken the other fork. That is to say, they have understood the play of the real world, with all of its suffering, not in simple terms of "nature red in tooth and claw" but through the celebration of the gift-exchange quality of our give-and-take. "What a big potlatch we are all members of!" It is allowing the sacred to enter and accepting the sacramental aspect of our shaky temporary personal being. (PW, 20)

Yes, what a big potlatch it is! It is the grand communion of all life.[5] Contemporary research has discovered that the many genes found in our bodies, perhaps even the majority of them, are not even human, but rather foster the myriad life forms (bacteria) that make even the *communion* of our own bodies possible.

In the big potlatch, no one is originally excluded, but given the obsessions of the Modern Constitution, many of us have no awareness of the great underlying potlatch whose various bioregional permutations are the possibility of any kind of life. It is as if we sleepwalk through it. "Gift economy? That might be another perspective on the meaning of ecology. We are living in the midst of a great potluck at which we are all invited guests. And we are also eventually the meal" (BF, 34). We could say here that potlatch is a way of naming ecology after the end of the Modern Constitution, that is, after the end of the separation of science and value. I here take up the possibility of awakening to wise and compassionate membership, however imperfectly enacted, in the great potlatch of earth democracy (the science of ecology *inseparable from* the spirituality, ethics, and politics of earth democracy). For those who dwell on Turtle Island (or elsewhere):

> Another indicator is the local "song and dance." The occasion of singers, musicians, storytellers, mask makers, and dancers joining together is the flow of daily life. Not only the human is danced, but raven, deer, cow, and rainstorm make their appearance. The dance enables us to present our many human and nonhuman selves to each other, and to place. The place is offered to itself. Art and economics are both matters of gift-exchange and the dance offering in particular has been a proper sort of trade for the taking of fruits, grain, or game. Such giving also helps us overcome our tendencies toward stinginess and arrogance. (PW, 53–54)

Indeed, Snyder tells us, "of all moral failings and flaws of character, the worst is stinginess of thought, which includes meanness in all its forms" (PW, 22). How does the potlatch offer the place to itself and thereby enable us to overcome our stingy ego selves?

III

Snyder's relatively youthful text, *Earth House Hold* (1969), is filled with extraordinary claims whose unintentional humor stems from their capacity to expose our persistently stingy modes of social organization. As he defends the "tribal" modes that characterized more archaic modes of community, he claims that "the modern American family is the smallest and most barren family that has ever existed" (EHH, 110). Amid the cold war and the rise of the military industrial complex, Snyder notes the "super hunting bands of mercenaries like Rand or CIA may in some ways belong to the future, if they can be transformed by the ecological conscience, or acid [LSD], to which they are very vulnerable" (EHH, 111). He defends the flourishing of Rinzai and Sōtō Zen practice in North America, noting that "many of the newcomers turned to traditional meditation after initial acid experience" (EHH, 109). Indeed, everywhere Snyder extols the power of a "Great Subculture"[6] and its opposition to the "Civilization Establishment" and the "State," which Snyder characterizes as "greed made legal" (GSR, 43). The subculture of the 1960s, as do all subcultures, "had its roots 40,000 years ago" (RW, 68).

While experimentation with mind-altering drugs can break the hegemonic hold of our manufactured mind, continued use after its initial capacity to shock us into awakening may be difficult to sustain. (Snyder remains happy that he quit when he was ahead.) It is a bit like Plato's prisoner who suddenly finds herself in the stacked deck of the Cave: the manufacture of the real has been exposed. One comes to see that the so-called free world is inhabited by hungry ghosts or *preta*, who are cursed with both enormous appetites and little necks that continuously thwart their avaricious consumption, making them even more avaricious (EHH, 91). Paths out of the cave and out of the dusty realm of ghosts have always been difficult to activate. Today "the prevailing ideology of capitalism—that we are by our nature greedy and enslaved to our innate interests—writes off practices of transformation as idealistic fantasies." Yet the goal of practice is more than the dawning clarity that the mind has been duped by prevailing hegemonic interests: the "goal of Revolution is Transformation" (EHH, 128). For Snyder this included the practice of Zazen, which allows us to break the ideological stranglehold of modernity and begin to recover and transform archaic traces of the Great Subculture.

This is not to abandon the so-called prison of Western thought for a supposedly awakened Asian thought. No language, culture, time, or person owns the Dharma. "The 'truth' in Buddhism and Hinduism is not dependent in any sense on Indian or Chinese culture; and that 'India' and 'China'—as societies—are as burdensome as any others; perhaps more so. It became clear that 'Hinduism' and 'Buddhism' as social institutions had long been accomplices of the State in burdening and binding people, rather than serving to liberate them. Just like the other Great Religions" (EHH, 114). Snyder always defends the insurgent and liberating practices within any religion and practice, including those within the Judeo-Christian-Islamic tradition, as part of the long alternative history of the Great Subculture.

Although to activate transformative practice is to learn to dwell in and as your place, it is nonetheless also an awakening as wide as the Great Earth. "Beings are numberless and I vow to free them all," proclaims the mad generosity of the first of the four bodhisattva vows, itself a transformation of the more ego-centered initial formulation of the Buddha's first noble truth, namely the truth of *duḥkha* or the disharmonious rut of insatiable desire. Nonetheless, Snyder also realized early on that this is quite far from the *actual* social and political achievements of Buddhism, which has developed techniques that have only liberated a relatively small number of assiduous practitioners (and even then, as we saw in chapter 2, with a clear and scandalous gender bias). "Institutional Buddhism has been conspicuously ready to accept or ignore the inequalities and tyrannies of whatever political system it found itself under. This can be death to Buddhism, because it is death to any meaningful function of compassion. Wisdom without compassion feels no pain" (EHH, 90). Indeed, the "monstrous protection rackets" (EHH, 91) of contemporary world politics cannot be ignored if the Dharma is going to be anything more than a personal vocation that, as such, is inadvertently complicit with global capitalism. For Snyder, transformative practice, Zen, pagan, tribal, Judeo-Christian-Islamic, or what have you, means "supporting any cultural and economic revolution that moves clearly toward a free, international, classless world" (EHH, 92).

The way forward, however, does not just go directly forward; it opens to the future through a radical retrieval, renewal, and reimagination of the past. "The tribe, it seems, is the newest development in the Great Subculture. We have almost unintentionally linked ourselves to a transmission of gnosis, a potential social order, and techniques of enlightenment, surviving from prehistoric times" (EHH, 116).

IV

Discourses that are animated by indigenous or tribal sources, indeed the very notion of tribal Dharma itself, are sometimes criticized for being an appropriation or colonization, or even outright theft, of such sources. After the cataclysm wrought upon indigenous peoples, stories are among the few precious things that they still have and the White Man, even the well-meaning one, comes in and takes that, too. Sometimes this is the condescension that assumes that we can tell indigenous peoples what they really think and what these stories really mean. Or we may just take their stories, bereft of context, and retell them with no real curiosity about the world out of which we wrenched them. Or, worst of all, we just make up self-serving stories and attribute them to indigenous people to give them the veneer of authenticity.

After winning the Pulitzer Prize for *Turtle Island*, Snyder was criticized by some indigenous leaders and writers (Leslie Marmon Silko and others)[7] for assuming that he could speak for the real (nonwhite) indigenous people. Should they not speak for themselves? Do we not have other responsibilities to indigenous peoples? Yes, they should and, of course, we do. Clearly more prizes, Pulitzer and otherwise, should have gone to indigenous works and their authors and clearly they merit our careful attention. The rise of white new age shamans of all sorts should still give us pause. When listening to the stories that belong to a place, one should do so humbly and with big, patient, generous ears. When indigenous Elders solicit our attention and tell us that they have some things to teach us, we should be grateful and listen carefully. On the other hand, *Turtle Island* in particular and Snyder's work in general are both a thoroughgoing expropriation of the inhabitory regimes of white privilege and a practice of solidarity with all beings. Snyder does not speak *for* indigenous peoples but rather *with* them.

An audience member at a public interview in New York City in 1992 reported that his teacher, a Lakota, had claimed that Snyder was an Indian. "Ask him if he knows it" and that is what the audience member did. "Do you know that you are an Indian? A Native American" (GSR, 336)? Snyder's response is instructive:

> That was very kind of her to say that. I don't know if I'm an Indian or not. However, I do know that I'm a Native American. Here again is a Turtle Island bioregional point. Anyone is, metaphorically speaking, a Native American who is "born again on Turtle Island." Anyone is a Native American who chooses, consciously and deliberately, to live on this continent. (GSR, 336)

Eliot Weinberger pressed him further: "But do you think that the myths that come out of here belong to everyone" (GSR, 336)? Snyder responded that "they belong to the place, and they will come to belong to those who make themselves members of this place" (GSR, 337). Weinberger persisted, continuing to play the devil's advocate, reminding Snyder that in the 1970s some Native Americans had criticized him for allegedly appropriating their stories and images, including the image and stories of the Trickster Coyote. Snyder responded that these stories have versions that are widely distributed, often all over the human world. Even when they are relatively local, however, the power of these stories has already begun to penetrate the literary and philosophical consciousness of Turtle Island. "You can't be against it. It makes both worlds, the old and new, richer, and it testifies to the openness of the imagination" (GSR, 337). This is a critical point: the goal is not to strip Native American cultures of even more of their culture nor is it to tell them who they are. They are perfectly able to speak eloquently and powerfully for themselves. It is we who have to deepen our listening practices, extending them to the *upāya* that belong to place.[8]

When European settlers came to Turtle Island, it was a feeding frenzy and folks took whatever they wanted. *Appropriation is the mode of the original habitation*. The obsession with appropriation is to inhabit a place without in any way becoming present to that place. Re-inhabitation, however, is to be "born again on Turtle Island" and it is therefore to hear it as the "new-old name for the continent." To hearken to the "voice of nature herself, whom the ancient poets called the great goddess, the Magna Mater" (TI, 107), who awakens as Tārā, is to overcome oneself and be reborn as the place that gives one to oneself. This demands an end to lopsided consumption and reckless appropriation. We *are* our place, but the place is not merely surrounding us—it is not lying about, waiting for us to take whatever we want. "So it's time for Americans to grow up and BE here (BF, 18). Re-inhabitation is to enter the potlatch of place, with its potlatch of places and Indra's net of palaces without end, old and new.

In "The Hump Backed Flute Player" (from *Mountains and Rivers Without End*), we hear:

Ghost bison, ghost bears, ghost bighorns, ghost lynx, ghost pronghorns, ghost panthers, ghost marmots, ghost owls, swirling and gathering, sweeping down, in the power of a dance and a song.

Then the white man will be gone. (MR, 82)

When the spirits of place—most now threatened or extinct and reduced to ghosts—return in the Potlatch of Place, the white man dies. This is done in part through the enactment of the Nanissáanah or Ghost Dance received in a dream vision during the solar eclipse in 1889 by a Northern Paiute shaman from the Great Basin called Wovoka (and called Jack Wilson by those who did not reside on Turtle Island). Repetition of the five-day Nanissáanah would bring the spirits of the living and the dead together and end the white man's predatory expansion.[9] In an explanatory footnote, Snyder carefully clarifies that "white man" is "not a racial designation, but a name for a certain set of mind. When we all become born again-again natives of Turtle Island, then the 'white man' will be gone" (MR, 149).[10] White symbolizes the "invader's mentality" but invaders can come in all colors. "It doesn't matter what color your skin is, it's a matter of how you relate to the land" (RW, 86). Because there is little hope that our corporate politicians and overlords will ever practice Zazen, perhaps somebody needs to give them peyote and take them on a vision quest.

Re-inhabitation is to learn to listen carefully (HWH, x) and to "hear with a whole mind" (HWH, xv) as Robert Bringhurst, the great Canadian poet and translator of Haida stories, said of Snyder's earliest extant work, his undergraduate thesis on the Haida story, "The Man Who Hunted Birds in the Village." Snyder has claimed that many of the themes that have occupied him over the last six decades were originally foreshadowed in this thesis, which, despite its youthful voice, holds up nicely. (Snyder from early on was attracted to women who married bears and, as we see in his thesis, to men who married geese.) Introducing a new edition of this work, Snyder remarked that "old tales and myths and stories are the *kōans* of the human race" (HWH, xviii).[11] The ancient stories and life ways, a mode of access that Snyder calls Original Mind, can still tell us "how to be in some specific ecosystem of the far-flung world" (HWH, xviii).

Perhaps we could think of the Great Earth, as Snyder does, as the *kōan* of the Big Potlatch of which we are all members. *Potlatch* derives from Chinook Jargon (a pidgin trade language first used in the Lower Columbia in what is now Washington and Oregon, and which spread widely throughout the Salish Sea, up into modern British Columbia, Alaska, and even the Yukon).[12] It likely derives from the Nootka words for giving and gift, meaning finally to "transfer property in the context of a public feast" and hence "in effect . . . to buy status."[13] There were many variations of potlatch but at their heart, Bringhurst notes, here speaking of the Haida *waahlghal* potlatch, they were "public alterations to the person: the assumption of new names, receiving of tattoos, or piercing of the septum, lip or ears. All such quantum leaps in personal identity require publication and acceptance" (SSK, 286).

If this were just a local exchange of goods—commodities for a promotion in social rank—why did Canadian and U.S. missionaries and politicians push so hard to abolish it? Douglas Cole sites several reasons, but the most important among them was an economic reason:

> The system was based on the hoarding of goods, not for savings or investment, but for seemingly senseless waste. "It is not possible,"

wrote Indian Commissioner G. M. Sproat, "that Indians can acquire property, or become industrious with any good result, while under the influence of this mania."[14]

Potlatch was the "mania" in which the public rank or value of one's self was not part of the rational economic maintenance of one's self-interest. Gary Snyder as a young college student cited Ruth Benedict's assessment of potlatch as "Dionysian" and "megalomaniac-paranoid by Western standards," noting that "the ultimate reason why a man of the Northwest Coast cared about the nobility titles, the wealth, the crests, and the prerogatives lays bare the mainspring of their culture; they used them in a contest in which they sought to shame their rivals" (HWH, 16). Snyder describes a typical Haida potlatch:

> The house potlatch, the most spectacular and important of Haida festivals, required property that sometimes took fifteen years to collect. Besides being the occasion of several months of storytelling, dancing, ceremonial acting, and new status announcement, it finally resulted in the group construction of a large new house. This project was climaxed with the ceremonial raising of the totem pole—carved by imported, hired craftsmen—with a slave sometimes placed at the bottom of the hole to be crushed by the weight of the sliding pole as a final sign, on the owner's part, of his utter disdain of wealth. In the light of this and other occasionally destructive acts, we see the Haida goal not to be wealth in itself, but the prestige that can be gained by shaming and overwhelming others by the distribution of it. (HWH, 26)

Given the deep and pervasive hold that capitalism has on us—it is easier to imagine the destruction of the earth through climate change than an alternative to capitalism—it is hard to imagine prestige based not on wealth but on the radical expenditure of wealth. On this point, Georges Bataille's famous "economic" analysis of potlatch remains instructive. One cannot understand the great potlatch, that is, the ceremony that invites other clans to witness the power of superior gift-giving (the giving away of vast amounts of wealth that have been acquired, often over a long period of time, in order to secure rank), within the paradigm of a classical form of exchange. One is not, in some very profound sense, actually *purchasing* rank. One vanquishes one's rival by demonstrating a superior level of generosity, by exceeding any rival's capacity to dispose of as much wealth in the form of gifts. How does one profit from loss? "He enriches himself with a contempt for riches, and what he proves to be miserly of is in fact his generosity."[15]

The potlatch, at least implicitly, enacts the ultimate impossibility of wealth being something that *I own*. How does one profit—adequately pay off the witnesses for the acquisition of rank—when the price of rank is to win a rivalry of generosity, a rivalry, Bataille notes, in which somehow "loss is changed into acquisition" (AS, 74). This has long been Snyder's sense of the feast, of communion, *puja*, and potlatch. Poetry—clear, penetrating, generous, compassionate—is far more powerful than fossil fuels and nuclear energy. "The power within—the more you give, the more you will have to give—will still be our source when coal and oil are long gone, and atoms are left to spin in peace" (TI, 114).

The general economy of potlatch is not in the end really acquisitive, and the missionaries were right, despite their horror, to see in it a ritual that has nothing to do with barter, that supposedly originary economic—and pernicious—myth about the earliest forms of wealth enhancement. Despite the fact that the immense fraud that is the movement of global capital seems to be in our bones, original forms of wealth (the cultivation of noble, powerful, wise, compassionate ways of life) are not first and foremost things for which one can haggle. Potlatch does not barter material goods in exchange for rank in some sort of quid pro quo because the disposal of wealth, that is, the ostentatious gift (witness paying) does not result in the gaining of anything. Rank—the putative "owning" of no thing—is not itself really a useful thing. The capacity to disown all that would be or could be commodified results in a wealth that defies commodification. As Snyder observed the same insight at play in some parts of Polynesian culture: The "Big Person, the most respected and powerful figure in the village, was the one who had nothing—whatever gift came to him or her was promptly given away again. This is the real heart of a gift economy, an economy that would save, not devour, the world" (BF, 34–35). It is a wealth beyond *owning* wealthy things and in this sense, Bataille tells us, "*rank* is the opposite of a thing: What founds it is sacred. . . . It is the stubborn determination to treat as a disposable and usable *thing* that whose essence is sacred, that which is completely removed from the profane utilitarian sphere . . . " (AS, 73).

Indeed, the profit of rank "withdraws wealth from productive consumption" (AS, 76). One could, and here it is worthwhile to recall Snyder's own economic modesty, come to appreciate being born again into a realm of wealth that has nothing to do with the acquisitive and inhabitory ego and its regimes of increasingly corporate wealth production. What could only be regarded as poverty in the economic exchanges that comprise the inhabitory ideology of capitalism is in the potlatch an awakening to genuine wealth, a wealth that has nothing to do with a consumer amassing commodities. The rich are poor—starving hungry ghosts—because they can only bring money and stuff to the table. "In this respect," Bataille concludes, "present-day society is a huge counterfeit, where this *truth* of wealth has underhandedly slipped into *extreme poverty*. The true luxury and the real potlatch of our times falls to the poverty stricken, that is, to the individual who lies down and scoffs" (AS, 76). Capitalism is a fraud, a stingy manner of communion and exchange that invites a hearty scoff. As Snyder later reintroduced his senior thesis on the Haida story "He Who Hunted Birds in His Father's Village," he expressed his own potlatch scoff: "A curse on monocultural industrial civilization and its almost deified economic and political systems that compete, exploit, and then give vast wealth and power to a tiny few while draining and scattering the cultural and natural wealth of our planet" (HWH, xix).

V

One could also appreciate the manner in which the tribal Dharma of the Big Potlatch resonates with what some Mahāyāna Sūtras call the Gathering of the Assembly or the Assembly of all Buddhas, that is, the Great Saṅgha of the earth comprised of all sentient beings. One could here speak of something like a Potlatch Saṅgha, and in so doing, note that Snyder's writing career began with a marriage potlatch, in this case, a young Haida man who fell in love with a beautiful young Canadian Goose, who, like most all animals, could temporarily take off her skin and appear human. She ate no human food at the great wedding potlatch, but she continued to eat the small edible roots (*tc!āl*) typically found at the mouths of creeks, a food she later shared with the village when other food was scarce. She was eventually mocked for thinking so highly of goose food—she was not considered one of them; she did not properly belong to the group. She promptly departed, leaving her husband disconsolate. He eventually went on a great quest, meeting many hybrid creatures, and then ascended a huge pole to a kingdom in the sky where he found his wife and lived again with her as her husband. Alas, he soon grew to dislike living in this strange new kingdom. Raven eventually tried to carry him back to his human home, but at the last minute grew tired and the husband fell to the reef, becoming a seagull.

The early turn to a tale about the marriage of a Haida man to a Canadian Goose links four decades later to Snyder's retelling (in *The Practice of the Wild*) of an Athabaskan story of a marriage between a woman and a bear. Both stories come to us from anthropological data collections—Maria Johns of the Tlingit and Athabaskan speaking peoples of southern Yukon Territory reporting to the anthropologist Catherine McClellan in 1948 and the great blind Haida storyteller Ghandl (of the Qayahl Llaanas, born c. 1851) reporting to John Reed Swanton in 1900; both were also collected as artifacts during periods of calamitous cultural upheaval. As such, they were transmitted bereft of their original ritual contexts (performance, music, ceremony, clan and moiety affiliation, etc.). It is not difficult to appreciate that these generally denigrated lifeways and poetic storytelling traditions remain very fragile, as does the ecology of the earth itself. Where are the stories and poetries and philosophies of the Wild that help us to understand the places that comprise and constitute us? These stories continue to have at best a marginal relationship to the great inhabitory regimes. In the insularity of the latter, however, we are not present to the Dharma Potlatch that is our intermarriage with the nonhuman earth. In 1969 Snyder noted that,

> Animal marriages (and supernatural marriages) are a common motif of folklore the world around. A recent article by Lynn White puts the blame for the present ecological crisis on the Judeo-Christian tradition—animals don't have souls and can't be saved; nature is merely a ground for us to exploit while working out our drama of free will and salvation under the watch of Jehovah. (EHH, 122)

Snyder's letter exchange with Wendell Berry indicates that he is open to alternate readings and retrievals of the resources inherent in the scriptures of the various peoples of the Book. They, too, are members of the Dharma Potlatch; but it is also important to develop a new/old variation of Original Mind (sometimes called Indigenous Mind) as part of the awakening practice of reinhabitation. Of course, the more administratively oriented anthropologists and our sober-minded bureaucrats would respond to this account of potlatch much like the early missionaries responded to the ceremony itself: it is a reprehensible and irresponsible mania. To this I respond that it is indeed a story (*upāya*), but a story as sharp as a knife. "The *indigenas* are bearers of the deepest insights into human nature, and have the best actual way to live, as well. May this be realized before they are destroyed" (HWH, xix). The maniacal position is to call the Earth Potlatch—our shared home after all—maniacal.

❦ 6 ❧

Seeds of Earth Democracy

The Blue Sky

is the land of

OLD MAN MEDICINE BUDDHA

where the Eagle

that Flies out of Sight

flies. (MR, 45)

I

Snyder "was once told by a Native California elder that the diagnostic and healing hand of a 'trembling-hand healer's hand' was guided by an eagle so high up in the sky as to be out of sight" (MR, 162). This is the healing of emptiness (the nonplace in every place) and the manifestation of Tārā (recalling again that the glyph for sky is the same as the glyph for *śūnyatā*, emptiness). The Buddha, embodied in the blue medicine Buddha, blue like lapis lazuli and the deep blue sky,[1] considered his teachings not so much as theories or philosophioal arguments but as a box of medicine. The healing of place is to go deep into emptiness, unleashing the wisdom of awakening and the compassion of emptiness. This is the site where the Buddha and the shaman converge. To be clear: Snyder is not engaged in the fantasy that he is an indigenous shaman and is not trying to steal that role away from indigenous peoples. The figure of the shaman is one of the buddhas already to be found on Turtle Island and Snyder allows it to create a space of healing that allows for the return of Turtle Island, the sailing of a new Pequod no longer squandering the biodiversity and cultural diversity of Turtle Island on conquest.

The Buddha-shaman is both something archaic and something brand new, an advent of a new-old place of reinhabitation. Snyder is trying, as Charles Molesworth once put it, "to imagine more far-reaching harmonies while preseving all the wealth of the past."[2] In order to help the healing of place, we must must first heal the virulence that we do to ourselves and that *is* ourselves. The Buddha-shaman has "particular specialized powerful healing songs" and they "make a special point of going back into solitude for more songs: which will enable them to heal" (RW, 171).[3] The "poet as myth-handler-healer" (RW, 172) returns human life anew to the Wild *without* (the bioregions of the Great Earth, the meeting of the bottomless depth of the earth and the infinite expanse of the sky) and *within* (the Wild of our own minds and languages). Healing, which is always "just begun" (RW, 173), detoxifies the defiled emotions or *kleśas*—what Snyder glossed as "obstacles, poisons, mixed-up feelings, mean notions, angriness, sneaky exploitations" (RW, 137). Clearing our mind and opening our heart—whether we "'meditate and follow the Buddha Dharma' or 'Work well and have gratitude to Mother Earth,'"—"we're getting at these poisons; that's what the shaman's healing song is all about" (RW, 137). Healing clarifies anew the original mind, or indigenous mind, or Buddha mind, who we were before our parents were born. "I think the poet articulates the semi-known for the tribe. This is close to the ancient function of the shaman" (RW, 5). This is the paradoxical temporality at the heart of healing: to remember in a new way what you did not know that you ever knew.

II

In the contemporary world where more is never enough, Snyder reflected on the unspoken motto of his Rinzai training: "Grow with Less" (TI, 104). Yet it is the legions of hungry ghosts (*preta*) that seem to grow unabated. In "Tomorrow's Song" from *Turtle Island* we hear the following:

> The USA slowly lost its mandate
> in the middle and later twentieth century
> it never gave the mountains and rivers,
>   trees and animals,
>   a vote.

> all the people turned away from it
> > myths die; even continents are impermanent
>
> Turtle Island returned.
> my friend broke open a dried coyote-scat
> removed a ground squirrel tooth
> pierced it, hung it
> from the gold ring
> in his ear.
>
> We look to the future with pleasure
> we need no fossil fuel
> get power within
> grow strong on less. (TI, 77)

In the almost four decades since Snyder wrote these words, this future seems less and less nigh and Snyder's resolve reveals its Zen fortitude rather than is prognostic prowess. The environmental degradation against which Snyder has protested his whole life continues its mad and unabated plunge into ruin. The ongoing "war against the imagination,"[4] which manifests for Snyder as overpopulation (PS, 32–34), pollution (PS, 34–38), and overconsumption (PS, 38–41), has resulted in malignancies like deforestation and habitat loss, the decimation of biodiversity, global warming, the catastrophic earth-wide compromise of ecosystems, the extinction of native cultures and their ways, and the "loss of heart and soul" (PS, 59). Snyder later confessed in 1995 that "the apprehension that we felt in 1969 has not abated" (PS, 46):

> Many of the larger mammals face extinction, and all manner of species are endangered. Natural habitat ("raw land") is fragmented and then destroyed ("developed"). The world's forests are being relentlessly logged by multinational corporations. Air, water, and soil are all in worse shape. Population continues to climb, and even if it were a world of perfect economic and social justice, I would argue that ecological justice calls for fewer people. The few remaining traditional people with place-based sustainable economies are driven into urban slums and cultural suicide. The quality of life for everyone everywhere has gone down, what with resurgent nationalism, racism, violence both random and organized, and increasing social and

economic inequality. There are whole nations for whom daily life is an ongoing disaster. (PS, 46)

If the "few remaining traditional people with place-based sustainable economies" are rapidly disappearing, how does one sing a song "with pleasure" for the "return of Turtle Island"? Given that such a future is a *revolutionary non sequitur* from our prevailing sense of place, indeed, from our very self-understanding, how does one sing to a future that we mainly experience as in its death knell?

Early in his adult life, Snyder moved from the Pacific Northwest back to San Francisco and lived in the then multiethnic—"totally non-Anglo" (PS, 3)—Bohemian neighborhood of North Beach. He and the poets of the so-called San Francisco Renaissance belonged to "one of those few times in American history that a section of the population has freely chosen to disaffiliate itself 'from the American standard of living' and all that goes with it" (PS, 10). Before the rise of the Transamerica Pyramid, "a strikingly wasteful and arrogant building" (PS, 4), and the now current transformation of the neighborhood into another playground for IT millionaires, for all its flaws and failures, this was a place for the "good work of hatching something *else* in America; pray it cracks the shell in time. Gratitude to the Spirits of the Place; may all beings flourish" (PS, 6). *How does such a shell crack? How do the Spirits of the Place manifest when place itself has become a site of domination and the imposition of ego?* The relentless gentrification not only of North Beach, but also of San Francisco as a whole, may have driven North Beach to the same kind of fate as the "few remaining traditional people with place-based sustainable economies," but the work of the awakening of place continues unabated: "may all beings flourish."

The cracking of the shell, "forming the new society within the shell of the old" (RW, 169), releasing not only Turtle Island but all of the myriad Spirits of Place in the all of the many places that are the Great Earth, demands the cracking of the shell by which, in delusionally supposing that we are ourselves (that we are in ownership of an isolatable and self-standing self), we appropriate place as our property. The cracking of this shell is what NISHITANI Keiji cherished, following the great Hakuin and others, as the cultivation of the Great Doubt and the Great Death. Not to be confused with the Cartesian Doubt, which doubts everything but itself (the most dubitable and pernicious delusion of all), the Great Doubt, omnivorously devouring each and every habit of thought, occasions the Great Death, which is not the termination of our mortal coils, but the death of the self as a fixed point of reference. "It is like the bean whose seed and shell break apart as it ripens: the shell is the tiny ego, and the seed the infinity of the Great Doubt that encompasses the whole world. It is the moment in which the self is at the same time the nothingness of self." And hence Zen pronounces: "In the Great Death heaven and earth become new and that by which heaven and earth are born anew." This is not the revelation of some new thing, but an opening to the horizon of presentation as such, "the true reality of the self and things, in which everything is present just as it is, in its *suchness*."[5]

It is not that place and its spirits are hiding and that we need to discover them. In the *Vimalakīrti Sūtra*, the Buddha declared that "when the mind is pure, the Buddha land will be pure." Śāriputra was confused: if the world must be purified, does that mean that it is originally impure—that the Pure Land is somehow originally impure? And given that the Buddha's mind was pure, how could the world have been impure? The Buddha responded, "Are the sun and the moon impure? Is that why the blind man fails to see them?"[6] Or as the Chinese *tenzo* [monastery chef] famously clarified to Dōgen: *everywhere, nothing hidden*. Or as Snyder himself approvingly cited Dōgen to his friend, Wendell Berry: "when the ten thousand things come forward and verify you, that is enlightenment but when you go forward and verify the ten thousand things, that is delusion."[7]

We live at an increasingly global level within the shell of an earth covered up by our going forth and verifying the ten thousand things, a world where all places are becoming a dispirited and claustrophobic world of a single place, the many for a few (the "ten thousand" at the disposal of a single species and most members of that species at the disposal of a miniscule amount of its members). The earth is increasingly becoming a dispirited place where none of the ten thousand things has a vote, not even the full cultural range and ecological diversity of our own species. What then of Turtle Island? What of these displaced Spirits of Place? What is this call to earth democracy? As Vandana Shiva has argued:

> In contrast to viewing the planet as private property, movements are defending, on a local and global level, the planet as a commons. In contrast to experiencing the world as a global supermarket, where goods and services are produced with high ecological, social, and economic costs and sold for abysmally low prices, cultures and communities everywhere are resisting the destruction of their biological and cultural diversity, their lives, and their livelihoods. As alternatives to the suicidal, globalized free market economy based

on plundering and polluting the earth's vital resources, which displaces millions of farmers, craftspeople, and workers, communities are resolutely defending and evolving living economies that protect the life on earth and promote creativity.[8]

Shiva argues that "corporate globalization" moves in the opposite direction of earth democracy. The latter seeks the inclusivity of the whole Great Earth while the former "is based on new enclosures of the commons; enclosures which imply exclusions and are based on violence" (ED, 2). Indeed, "commons are the highest expression of economic democracy" (ED, 3). For Snyder, the household or *oikos* (οἶκος) at the heart (and in the etymology) of economy is the Great Earth itself, and it includes all beings. In our present context, we could say that earth democracy requires the opening and cultivation of a kind of true Dharma eye capable of double vision, seeing and analyzing both the dust of the delusional global corporate *sahāloka* and the many manifestations of the breaking through of the coming of the Buddha lands.

In this respect I here recall undergoing a daylong retreat with Ruben Habito dedicated to opening up a space of awakening in and between Zen and Ignatius' *Spiritual Exercises*. Among the participants was a Swinomish Elder who confided to me that he could not fully celebrate the beauty of the grounds of the retreat center in particular or of the greater Seattle area in general, an area blessed with a fjord, a beautiful lake, towering mountains, bountiful produce, national parks, good coffee, and so on. "What I see is the sorrow," and he began to speak of his feelings of insurmountable and incalculable loss. He spoke not only of the desecration of his ancestral lands, but he also recounted his considerable efforts over the years to learn his own language in order to understand tape recordings made by the elderly last members of his language (a dialect of Salishan Lushootseed) and lands during the mid-twentieth century. They spoke knowing full well that they may have no audience; they spoke at the brink of the extinction of the Spirits of their Place. "I do not even know if I am worthy to mourn for them or if I am the one entitled to do so."

Yes, we live in the many lands of sorrow. To open our hearts to the sorrows of the earth like *Avalokiteśvara*, the bodhisattva of compassion who hears the sorrows of the world, can be shattering. Indeed, awakening to the Great Earth is the endeavor to become the Buddha sea that can receive and sustain all things, including all sorrows. But we must also remember that most people do not experience the hysterical ecstasies of consumerism at a mall or the mesmerism of "must watch" television as sorrow. To know the land of sorrow is to open the double vision that sees both the desecration and the promise of the Buddha lands, the profanation and the power of the Spirits of Place. "My small contribution to [Marxist] radical dialectic is to extend it to animals, plants: indeed, to the whole of life" (RW, 130).

III

I would here like to offer an example of such a double vision by turning to a small and, as such, deceptively inconsequential nation: Bhutan.

Written during the time of its unification, Bhutan's 1729 legal code proclaims, "If the Government cannot create happiness (*dekid*) for its people, there is no purpose for the Government to exist."[9] Well, that certainly has not stopped almost every other consequential government during the course of our species, but in 1972, the fourth king of Bhutan (Jigme Singye Wangchuck, who would eventually abdicate his throne in favor of a democratic government), replaced the GNP (an insanely ideological indicator of economic growth, willy-nilly, regardless of the nature or consequences of that growth) with the Gross National Happiness, which "measures the quality of a country in a more holistic way [than GNP] and believes that the beneficial development of human society takes place when material and spiritual development occurs side by side to complement and reinforce each other" (GNH, 6–7). The original four pillars of the GNH have recently expanded to nine (psychological well-being, standard of living, good governance, health, education, community vitality, cultural diversity and resilience, time use, and ecological diversity and resilience), and the Bhutanese bureaucracy, quixotic as it may be, even attempts to measure the status and progress of each of these pillars.

It is hard to imagine that the industrial world would ever care about the quality of our time (in the United States, worker productivity continues to increase while wages diminish), let alone many of these other values. It is difficult to imagine that the way we live promotes psychological well-being, even though there are certainly enclaves that seek to counter these trends. Yet as Snyder once told Paul Geneson: "a whole society *on the way* . . . is preferable to a fragmented, monastic transmission" (RW, 68).

It is, of course, easy to be cynical about little Bhutan and its less than 800,000 people. The case of the expulsion of the Lhotshampa, or "southerners," that is, the Nepali immigrants in the southern regions of Bhutan, putatively on the grounds that they refused to buy into Bhutan's policies, supposedly refutes the ambitions of the GNH. Traveling through Bhutan, one can see that itinerant Indian workers are building the many magnificent temples, stūpas (or chortens), and Buddhist universities and they do not appear to be robustly sharing in the GNH. Without belittling these issues, it is nonetheless important to remember that the GNH is a promise, an experiment, a vision of a different mode of living in an increasingly dispirited world. Chief among Bhutan's problems is the hysterical Western projection upon Bhutan, as if we sought to address the hell that we have made of our lives by continuously searching for a heavenly Shangri-La where these conditions did not obtain. When you visit Bhutan, one sees that they, too, struggle with many of the symptoms of human frailty. Walking through the streets of Thimpu, for instance, one sees rehabilitation services for alcohol and substance abuse. As someone I met in Thimpu confided, "Everywhere people deal with the same sorts of things. What is different here is just our attitude."

While the critical gesture is crucial to any dream of happiness, it is also important not to allow it to blossom into the kind of cynicism that immobilizes us. Awakening, the casting and falling away of the seed's hull, is not a consummate experience that obviates the hard work of philosophical, artistic, spiritual, scientific, anthropological, political, and economic thought. It is merely the promise that such tasks, infinite though they may be, can be done with an eye to the Spirits of Place. The coming of the Buddha lands is the ongoing movement of what Dōgen understood as the oneness and inseparability of practice-realization (*shushō-ittō*). Although we do not practice until it culminates in realization (the Buddha lands are already here), we nonetheless must awaken to the realization that we need to practice (and Zen or Buddhism more generally, with its 84,000 multifarious teachings, do not in any way exhaust the prospects for practice). For the seed to ripen and its hull to fall away, we must wake up to the need to cultivate the soil. During a meeting with Lopen (or teacher) Sangay Dorji Rinpoche, we were reminded that "if you want an apple tree, plant an apple seed. If you want a good effect, develop positive causes and conditions. If the seed is poison, the fruit will be poison." No one can make another happy any more so than we can legislate earth democracy into existence, but we can plant its seeds in the imperfect soils of our shared lives. No government can cause people to be happy. What policy makes us happy despite the realities of pain, sickness, old age, and death? As Aristotle already recognized in the *Nichomachean Ethics*, flourishing demands self-cultivation and one cannot altogether eliminate the impact of fortune (τύχη). Compassionate polices can, however, create more favorable conditions for the flourishing of all beings.

There are nineteen spoken languages in Bhutan, the overwhelming majority of which are threatened with extinction, just as the massive flora and fauna, including the snow leopard, of the Himalayas enjoys some of its last and exceedingly fragile refuge in this country. In its inevitably imperfect way, Bhutan understands that *all of its beings* belong to its democratic responsibility and that this responsibility in not merely to itself, but to what Dōgen called "the great earth without one speck of soil left out."

We could also reformulate the problem by looking briefly at another small and seemingly inconsequential country, El Salvador, a country with a turbulent and heartbreaking modern history. Although Snyder was raised by atheists and has a healthy and warranted suspicion of most all institutionalized forms of religion (including Christianity, especially its obsession with abortion in a world straining painfully under the burden of reckless overpopulation), he admires Christianity's strain of liberation theology and other like-minded social gospels. Because, as we saw in the previous chapter, Buddhists have tended to be too "quiescent," they "can learn from, or at least take note of, the section of the Church that is doing liberation theology" (NH, 39).

They would do well to take note of bodhisattvas like Fr. Ignacio Ellacuría, SJ, whose brains were blown out in 1989 by a U.S.-sponsored right wing death squad, along with five other Jesuits, their housekeeper, and her sixteen-year-old daughter. He spoke directly to this awakening. This was not only the country that had received $3.5 billion in U.S. military aid and which had murdered, often brutally, more than 70,000 civilians during a twelve-year-long civil war; it was also a country that still harbored a promise of consequence for the whole earth. Writing in the last year of life on the occasion of the quincentenary of the Spanish "discovery" of the Americas, Ellacuría distinguished discovery (*descrubrimiento*) from a cover-up (*encubrimiento*). When the Spanish "discovered" the Americas, they really covered them up and saw nothing but themselves. All that was discovered is "the reality of Spain, the reality of Western culture and also of the church of that time."[10] Indeed, "everything that was there was covered up, violently so. This profound cover-up gave way to a 'new culture,' to a 'new race,' to a 'new religion,' etc." (ELS, 33). As Snyder put it in his own way, we do not need to *re*discover Turtle Island. There was never a time that we had discovered it. In a different sense, we need to "*dis*-cover" it, that is, to remove the cover of our own nonseeing, to see *where* and thereby *who* we are with the true Dharma eye. "People live on it without knowing what it is or where they are. They live on it literally like invaders" (RW, 69).

Yet despite all of the deaths and violence, despite the fact that the U.S. embassy in San Salvador is now its second largest (after Baghdad), and despite the fact that the Central American Free Trade Agreement (CAFTA) has enabled the appropriation of the country as the spoils of war (a once strong agricultural economy reduced to mass unemployment and to eating imported processed foods, which must fight against Monsanto and fight for drinkable water and food security as human rights), Ellacuría had argued presciently that El Salvador still had the advantage, nay, even the "seed of liberation" (ELS, 37). Yes, the United States has a solution, but it is a "bad solution, both for them and for the world in general." On the other hand, Latin America has "no solutions, only problems; but as painful as they are, it is better to have problems than to have a bad solution for the future of history" (ELS, 34). The problematization of El Salvador and of Latin America more generally—the cover-up of its Spirits of Place so that it itself becomes the problem—has turned it, as the Spanish adage has it, into a "Christ," indeed, the figure of crucifixion itself. It was here that the Spirits of Place first returned, inhabiting figures like Archbishop Romero who had originally been chosen precisely for his somnolence, but whose "cleansed eyes saw the truth, and it was revealed to him what it means to be in apostle in El Salvador today" (ELS, 288). He could then see God in the "voiceless people"—he saw the crucified (covered-up) people and earth as "the path to arriving at a new heaven and a new earth" (ELS, 290).

Today we would have to say that the whole earth is being crucified—Pope Francis' earth as "burdened and laid waste" and, as such, "among the most abandoned and maltreated of our poor" (LS, 3).

IV

Earth democracy is impossible without the cultivation of a practice of peace. Reflecting on his work with the Buddhist Peace Fellowship, Snyder stated in 1985 that "it's part of our mission . . . as Buddhists to extend the concern for peace outside the human realm to the nonhuman realm."[11] This is not some Pollyannaish new age fantasy that one day the lamb really will lie down with the lion and that all creatures will transcend conflict, including the most conflict-addicted creature of all, we humans. As Snyder often reflects, nature has its dark and cruel aspects and the challenge is to affirm and love all of it, not just the parts that we prefer. Cultivating peace does not mean that one is always successful at achieving or maintaining it. Moreover, peace is not the same thing as pacification, a well-practiced weapon of war and domination. It is a question of *ahimsā*—nonviolence in the sense of doing "the least possible harm in every situation" (PS, 79), to avoid or oppose *hiṃsā*, injury, harm, violence. This is what Snyder also glosses as "respect for all beings"

(BF, 69). It is not the pipe dream of the end of all conflict;[12] it is rather a practice of the Wild that issues from an ongoing awakening that is shaped by wisdom and compassion, these mountains and rivers within and without that are without end.

> *Ahimsā* taken too literally leaves out the life of the world and makes the rabbit virtuous but the hawk evil. People who must fish and hunt to live can enter into the process with gratitude and care, and no arrogant assumptions of human privilege. This cannot come from "thinking about" nature; it must come from being within nature. (BF, 69)

It is to cultivate a sense of what Snyder more than four decades ago memorably dubbed the "great earth saṅgha" (TI, 73) or what he later called "the Mind of the Commons" (PW, 39). We act as if all of the forms of life that comprise our particular place matter because they do. All forms of resident life belong the constituency of a given place and all of the many places belong to the constituency of the earth.

> In Pueblo societies a kind of ultimate democracy is practiced. Plants and animals are also people, and, through certain rituals and dances, are given a place and a voice in the political discussions of the humans. They are "represented." "Power to all the people" must be the slogan. (TI, 104)

Pope Francis' "ecological conversion" would imply for Snyder "a new definition of humanism and a new definition of democracy that would include the nonhuman, that would have representation from those spheres. This is what I think we mean by an ecological conscience" (TI, 106). Bioregions are the dependent origination (*pratītyasamutpāda*) of people of all kinds, not just humans, and hence earth democracy grants personhood to all of the creatures whose manners of life make a place possible. It does so with the gratitude that we are part of that complexly interlocking gift of life and that doing our share for what grants us life is not merely our responsibility, but our joy.

> What we must find a way to do, then, is incorporate the other people—what the Sioux Indians called the creeping people, and the standing people, and the flying people, and the swimming people—into the councils of government. This isn't as difficult as you might

think. If we don't do it, they will revolt against us. They will submit non-negotiable demands about our stay on the earth. We are beginning to get non-negotiable demands right now from the air, the water, the soil. (TI, 108)

The Great Earth right now is asserting its radical powers of eminent domain to those who think that it belongs to them. In response earth democracy is a new way of understanding an ancient truth. "Hark again to those roots, to see our ancient solidarity, and then to the work of being together on Turtle Island" (TI, introductory note). Perhaps we could think of this as a radical expansion of John Rawls' original position: If you did not know which creature you would be, for which creatures would you advocate? You would be for all creatures.

Hence, the dawning of the Buddhist revolution for Snyder begins both with how one conducts one's own life and the sense of the Great Earth implicit in the politics and policies that one advocates on behalf of others. "Morality" in both cases ultimately moves "toward the true community (saṅgha) of 'all beings'" (EHH, 92). One could reframe our original position, beyond the self-interest implied in the Rawlsian version, in the form of the question that Patrick D. Murphy has posed: "What if we worked from a concept of relational difference and *anotherness* rather than Otherness?"[13] Far beyond Rawl's anthropocentric call to distributive justice, Snyder's Tārā-oriented justice—and compassion whose generosity and mercy exceed the more limited call of justice—asks us perhaps to take the myth of reincarnation more to heart. It is not that we may one day be another creature, but rather that we already have, at least in some metaphoric way, been all possible creatures. We should "take ourselves as no more and no less than another being in the Big Watershed. We can accept each other all as barefoot equals sleeping on the same ground" (PW, 24). Such non-separation is the root of earth democracy. "I am a child of all life, and all living beings are my brothers and sisters, my children and grandchildren" (TI, 93). In 1968, having returned from Japan and before getting the land on the San Juan Ridge upon which he would build Kitkitdizze, Snyder laughingly told Keith Lampe that he wanted to "get out there and agitate them trees and grasses into revolting against the exploiting class" (RW, 14).

Earth democracy is not pursued vaguely through some general appeal to the Great Earth. It occurs "place by place. Nature happens, culture happens, somewhere" (PS, 79). Even Kitkitdizze, the site of Gary Snyder's almost five decades of re-inhabitory practice, is just another "node in the net" (PS, 252).

This brings us to the paradox of the Great Earth and its many bioregions: the Great Earth can only be affirmed within a bioregion and as a bioregion.[14] Only by becoming mindful of ourselves as our place do we also participate in earth democracy. In "The Mountain Spirit," we hear of the capacity of a place that, in its liberation, reflects, like a node in Indra's net, the Great Earth itself.

> Ghosts of lost landscapes
>   herds and flocks,
>   towns and clans,
> great teachers from all lands
> tucked in Wovoka's empty hat,
>   stored in Baby Krishna's mouth,
>   kneeling for tea
> in Vimalakīrti's one small room. (MR, 148)

The great loss of biodiversity and cultural diversity, these returning spirits of place, are stored in Wovoka's hat (to be unleashed by the Ghost Dance). It is the infinite depths that could be seen when little dirt-eating Baby Krishna opened his mouth. It is the tiny little straw hat of the Tang Dynasty Chan Master Huangbo Xiyun (Jp. Ōbaku Keun), which, despite its size, contained the whole universe (MR, 165). It is the immense Great Assembly of all Buddhas who, instructed by the Buddha to learn what *upāya* Vimalakīrti was teaching by claiming to be ill, all magically convened in the little room around his sick bed. "No matter how many keep arriving, they all fit into his one small room, 'ten feet square'" (MR, 165). When there is a time of much sickness and therefore a need for great healing, Vimalakīrti will appear sick. Contained within the *upāya* of Vimalakīrti's sickness is the great healing. Clearing the mind and reading his sickness is like clearing the mind and reading the *Endless Streams and Mountains* scroll: within its very specific place (big hat, little straw hat, yawning baby mouth, sick body in a tiny room, a scroll in the Cleveland museum purchased with the profits from industry) *is* the Great Health of the Great Earth.

Snyder therefore modifies Joanna Macy and John Seed's call for a Council of All Beings by calling for a *"Village* Council of All Beings," which allows us to "get place-specific" (PS, 79). These village councils "would in some sense give all of these creatures voice. They would provide space for all" (PS, 80). One great Sangha with all of its bioregions, each made of the interpenetrating jewels of Indra and each in itself an interpenetrating jewel of Indra!

Turtle Island is, after all, "one ecosystem / in diversity / under the sun / with joyful interpenetration for all" (AH, 114).

It is easy to imagine that this vision of earth democracy will be dismissed as impractical and ineffective. This would be a cause of immeasurable sadness. Because the other alternatives do not attend to the root causes and conditions, to write off earth democracy is to resign oneself to the madness of the day. Perhaps that it is our fate, although every part of me hopes that this is not true. Nonetheless, we push on, attempting to be the change that we hope for the Great Earth, whether or not it comes about. "This is Zen. To give hundred percent and know it doesn't matter,"[15] explained Snyder in 1990.

Unperturbed and striving for the implacable resolve of Fudō Myō-ō, the Immovable Wisdom King, we harken to Snyder's "Gatha"—Sanskrit for verse or song and used *inter alia* in Buddhist sūtras—"for All Threatened Beings"

> Ah Power that swirls us together
> Grant us bliss
> Grant us the great release
> And to all beings
> Vanishing, wounded.
> In trouble on earth,
> We pass on this love
> May their numbers increase. (LOR, 175)

Notes

**Preface
(Milarepa's Stone Tower)**

1. This is from a letter in response to a question from the Dear Poets Commune. Quoted in Patrick D. Murphy, *A Place for Wayfaring: The Poetry and Prose of Gary Snyder* (2000), 10.

2. I have generally relied on the marvelous two-volume edition of the *Shōbōgenzō* edited by Kazuaki TANAHASHI (2010), 585. Except where custom prevails otherwise, I adhere to the East Asian custom of listing the family name first and in order to prevent confusion, I follow the custom of capitalizing the family name.

3. Paul Celan, "The Meridian," *Selected Poems and Prose of Paul Celan*, trans. John Felstiner (2001), 408. "Art creates I-distantness [*Ich-ferne*]" (406).

4. To "reject the world and opt entirely for spirit . . . has meant historically to neglect the biological and to really rip off nature consequently. Like puritanism does. Opts entirely for spirit and in its capitalist version allows for total exploitation of nature because nature is not particularly important" (RW, 89). "By the metaphor of 'spiritual cultivation' a holy man has weeded out the wild from his nature" (PW, 85). Indeed, traditional European ascetic practices were already sometimes a kind of "war against nature—placing the human over the animal and the spiritual over the human" (PW, 98).

5. Snyder also sometimes uses this word. For example, he tells us "what the spiritual path really is," namely, a maximization of our sense of community with a "shared practice of a set of values" (RW, 141).

6. Both *Inside Climate News* and the *Los Angeles Times* reported this story. Neela Banerjee, Lisa Song, and David Hasemyer, "Exxon: The Road not Taken: Exxon's Own Research Confirmed Fossil Fuels' Role in Global Warming Decades Ago," *Inside Climate News* (September 16, 2015); Sara Jerving, Katie Jennings, Masako Melissa Hirsch, and Susanne Rust, "What Exxon Knew about the Earth's Melting Arctic," *Los Angeles Times* (October 9, 2015).

7. Julia Martin pushed Snyder on this appellation and Snyder "wouldn't argue" (NH, 93).

8. "I think the poet articulates the semi-known for the tribe. This is close to the ancient function of the shaman" (RW, 5).

9. Snyder told Peter Barry Chowka that he had the formal vows of a Zen monk [presumably the Rinzai *tokudo-shiki*]: "my hair is long now simply because I have not shaved it lately. There is no role for a monk in the U.S." (RW, 99).

10. See Bret Davis's superb analysis of the *Fukanzazengi* generally as well as this point in general in "The Enlightening Practice of Nonthinking: Unfolding Dōgen's 'Fukanzazengi,' *Engaging Dōgen's Zen: The Philosophy of Practice as Awakening (Commentaries on Dōgen's "Shushōgi" and "Fukanzazengi")*, ed. Jason M. Wirth, Brian Schroeder, and Bret W. Davis (2017).

11. For an excellent reflection on Snyder's double-edged relationship to scholarship and books on the one hand and what he called "the real work" on the other hand, see Mark Gonnerman, "Fieldwork: Gary Snyder, Libraries, and Book Learning," in *A Sense of the Whole: Reading Gary Snyder's* Mountains and Rivers Without End, ed. Mark Gonnerman (2015), 291–315.

12. Francis H. Cook, *Hua-Yen Buddhism: The Jewel Net of Indra* (1977), 2.

13. "It's actually quite impossible to make any generalizations about history, the past or the future, human nature, or anything else, on the basis of our present experience. It stands outside the mainstream" (RW, 114).

14. As Snyder reflected in 1973: "I find it always exciting to me, beautiful, to experience the interdependencies of things, the complex webs and networks by which everything moves, which I think are the most beautiful awarenesses that we can have of ourselves and of our planet" (RW, 35).

15. David Landis Barnhill, "Great Earth *Saṅgha*: Gary Snyder's View of Nature as Community," *Buddhism and Ecology: The Interconnection of Dharma and Deeds* (1998), 189.

16. On the question of "whole earth thinking" as opposed to "global" thinking, see Sam Mickey's excellent study, *Whole Earth Thinking and Planetary Coexistence: Ecological Wisdom at the Intersection of Religion, Ecology, and Philosophy* (2016). "Global civilization spreads consumer culture everywhere, turning everything and everyone into resources, making everything look the same. Avoiding such homogenization, planetary civilization cultivates biological and cultural diversity, attending to all planetary beings on their own terms, each according to its own place" (8).

17. This complicity with the economics of the world also demands that the Buddhist right profession or right work is not merely to make your whole life a Sesshin [intensive period of Zazen practice], spending most all of your waking hours meditating. Work, including the growing and preparing of food, also has to become practice. "Sitting ten hours a day means that somebody else is growing your food for you; for special shots, okay, but people can't do it for a whole lifetime without somebody else having to give up their meditation so that *you* can meditate" (RW, 96). Taking time to practice Zazen is also learning to make one's life a many varied practice, "to steadily

pursue the unity of daily life and spiritual practice" (RW, 104). Or as Oda Sessō Rōshi taught Snyder: "In Zen there are only two things: you sit, and you sweep the garden. It doesn't matter how big the garden is" (RW, 119). We could say that this is the non-duality of right view [you sit] and right action [you sweep your garden/the big garden, you love your place/the Great Earth].

18. Pope Francis [Jorge Mario Bergoglio], *Encyclical Letter "Laudato Si'" of the Holy Father Francis: On Care for Our Common Home*. (2015). Henceforth LS.

19. Snyder quoted this to Wendell Berry. *Distant Neighbors: The Selected Letters of Wendell Berry and Gary Snyder*, ed. Chad Wriglesworth (2014), 73. Snyder is likely alluding to *Genjō Kōan*: "To carry the self forward and illuminate myriad things is delusion. That myriad things come forth and illuminate the self is awakening" ("Actualizing the Fundamental Point," S, 29).

20. American winners have included Rev. Gyomay Kubose in 1971, Mrs. Shinobu Matsuura in 1975, Rev. Hozen Seki in 1980, Dr. Kikuo Taira in 1984, Dr. Kenneth Inada in 1990, Gary Snyder in 1998, Dr. Alfred Bloom in 1999, Dr. Taitetsu Unno in 2006, and Dr. Barbara Ruch in 2008. The award is given under the auspices of the Bukkyō Dendō Kyōkai (The Society for the Promotion of Buddhism).

21. Gary Snyder with Eric Todd Smith, "'The Space Goes On': A Conversation about *Mountains and Rivers Without End*," in *A Sense of the Whole: Reading Gary Snyder's* Mountains and Rivers Without End, ed. Mark Gonnerman (2015), 274.

22. Snyder told Eric Todd Smith in 1998 in Kitkitdizze that our obsession with money, at the expense of all other values (time, quality of life) and our consequent overproduction, perhaps one could even say, our insanely rational devotion to economic efficiency as an end in itself, is the madness of the moment. "Until we break the stranglehold of that on the consciousness of culture—now it's gone all the way through the society—we're going to be nuts. We *are* nuts." Gary Snyder with Eric Todd Smith, "'The Space Goes On': A Conversation about *Mountains and Rivers Without End*," in *A Sense of the Whole: Reading Gary Snyder's* Mountains and Rivers Without End, ed. Mark Gonnerman (2015), 276.

23. *The Analects of Confucius: A Philosophical Translation*, trans. Roger T. Ames and Henry Rosemont Jr. (2010), 101.

Chapter 1
Mountains, Rivers, and the Great Earth

1. Some parts of this chapter appeared in a much different and shorter form as "Painting Mountains and Rivers: Gary Snyder, Dōgen, and the Elemental Sutra of the Wild," *Research in Phenomenology*, vol. 44 (2014), 240–261.

2. David Perkins, *A History of Modern Poetry: Modernism and After* (1987), 553. Henceforth HMP. To be fair, Perkins' commentary precedes the publication of many of Snyder's works that I discuss in this book. Moreover, there is no question

that Snyder allies himself with elements from traditions that are helpful to retrieve the Wild from its eclipse by the self-obsessed delusions of globalization.

3. In addition to being the title of Snyder's 1974 Pulitzer Prize–winning collection of poetry, Turtle Island is the "the new-old name" (TI, 105) for the North American continent used by the Haudenosaunee (Iroquois Confederacy) peoples and other Northeastern indigenous peoples. It has now spread widely as naming an alternative manner of inhabiting what we call North America. "Here is a generation of white people finally ready to learn from the Elders. How to live on the continent as though our children, and on down, will still be here (not on the moon). Loving and protecting this soil, these trees, these wolves. Natives of Turtle Island" (TI, 105).

4. The characters for "song after song" are sometimes read as referring to the eighty-four thousand verses, a classical way of evoking the immense breadth and variety of the Buddha's teaching, although it can also be heard as saying the immense breadth and variety of the Buddha Dharma, which is to say, to awaken to the infinite variegation and temporal impermanence of the whole earth without an inch of soil left out.

5. Gary Snyder, "On the Road with D. T. Suzuki," *A Zen Life: D. T. Suzuki Remembered*, ed. Masao ABE (1986), 207. The passage in Suzuki reads: "Before a man studies Zen, to him mountains are mountains and waters are waters; after he gets an insight into the truth of Zen through the instruction of a good master, mountains to him are not mountains and waters are not waters; but after this when he really attains to the abode of rest, mountains are once more mountains and waters are waters." D. T. Suzuki, *Essays in Zen Buddhism*, First Series (1926), 24. See also the discussion of this matter in Stephanie Kaza, "Heart to Heart: Instructions in Nonduality," in *A Sense of the Whole: Reading Gary Snyder's* Mountains and Rivers Without End, ed. Mark Gonnerman (2015), 247ff.

6. ABE Masao, *Zen and Western Thought*, ed. William R. LaFleur (1985), 4. For an excellent discussion of this in relationship to the issues at hand, see also Joan Qionglin Tan*, Han Shan, Chan Buddhism and Gary Snyder's Ecopoetic Way* (2009), esp. 56–61.

7. It is worth noting that even the explanatory Notes that conclude *Mountains and Rivers Without End* belong to its scroll structure—a structure that extends into the cosmic ecology of Indra's net while remaining deeply rooted in place. They are in themselves also experiments with *notes as poetry*, notes as part of an elemental and elementally awakened earth song.

8. "Someone at Page Street, I think, smuggled it to me" (MHM, 160). Page Street alludes to the San Francisco Zen Center. Bielefeldt wrote his MA thesis on *Sansui-kyō* in 1972 at UC Berkeley.

9. This inspired Graham Parkes to translate *Sansui-kyō* as "Mountains and Waters as Sūtras." See his introduction to this work in *Buddhist Philosophy: Essential Readings*, ed. William Edelglass and Jay L. Garfield (2009), 83–86.

10. Yamamba is a spectral manifestation (*yōkai*) of the mountains in the frequently performed and enduring Nō play of the same name. In the two-scene drama,

attributed to Zeami, she offers a traveler refuge in the mountain and asks that they perform the song and dance of the mountains in return. At the end of the play, it is the ancient and bedraggled Yamamba herself, who can shift like the clouds and for whom no mountain depth is inaccessible, who performs the dance. In Snyder's poem, we join in this dance: "The Mountain Spirit and me / like ripples of the Cambrian Sea / dance the pine tree . . . " (MR, 149).

11. For a more extended consideration of the problem of passage in general and in relationship to Schelling, see my *Schelling's Practice of the Wild: Time, Art, Imagination* (2015), chapter 3.

12. See ABE Masao's excellent discussion of this in his *A Study of Dōgen: His Philosophy and Religion*, ed. Steven Heine (1992), 81–88. Henceforth SD. I borrow the term unprethinkable, *unvordenklich*, from Schelling.

13. We have habituated ourselves to reserve value for the eternal, but the lack of eternal beings does not make them as such without value. Impermanence is "never a reason to let compassion and focus slide, or to pass off the sufferings of others because they are merely impermanent beings." As Issa observed, this is "but a dewdrop world." That is true. But Issa continues: "and yet—" and this for Snyder is the great matter. "That 'and yet' is our perennial practice. And maybe the root of the Dharma" (DP, 101–102).

14. "*Keisei Sanshoku* [Valley Sounds, Mountain Colors]," S, 89.

15. "*Shoaku Makusa* [Refrain from Unwholesome Action]," S, 97.

16. This translation of *Bendōwa* is from *The Heart of Dōgen's Shōbōgenzō*, trans. Norman Waddell and ABE Masao (2002). Henceforth HDS. See also *The Wholehearted Way: A Translation of Eihei Dōgen's* Bendōwa *with Commentary by Kōshō Uchiyama Rōshi*, trans. Shōhaku OKUMURA and Taigen Daniel Leighton (1997).

17. See also Dōgen's *Shōbōgenzō Zuimonki* [*Treasury of the True Dharma Eye: Record of Things Heard*], a collection of statements that Dōgen's beloved friend and Dharma heir, EJŌ Koun, is said to have heard Dōgen say: "When the Buddhas and the Patriarchs categorically state that the mind is plants and trees, revise your preconceptions and understand plants and trees as mind. If the Buddha is said to be tile and pebble, consider tile and pebble as the Buddha. If you change your basic preconceptions, you will be able to gain the Way." *A Primer of Sōtō Zen*, trans. Reihō MASUNAGA (1971), 66.

18. Hee-Jin Kim, *Dōgen Kigen: Mystical Realist* (1987), 187. Henceforth DKM.

19. Snyder acknowledges Sōkō MORINAGA as one of his three Dharma teachers in the "By Way of Thanks" section at the end of *Mountains and Rivers Without End* (MR, 166).

20. Katsunori YAMAZATO, "*Mountains and Rivers Without End* and Japanese Nō Theater," in *A Sense of the Whole: Reading Gary Snyder's* Mountains and Rivers Without End, ed. Mark Gonnerman (2015), 115.

21. Immanuel Kant, *Anthropology, History, and Education*, ed. and trans. Robert B. Louden and Günter Zöller (2008), 438.

22. "When you practice under a tree or in an open field, there is no toilet, so cleanse yourself with some dirt and water from a nearby river or valley brook. You may not find ash, so use two rows of seven pellets of dirt. . . . Also set up a stone for rubbing [for washing hands]. Then defecate, and afterward use a piece of wood or paper. When you are done, go to the water and cleanse yourself" (S, 51).

23. "Washing the face is not merely removing filth; it is the life vein of buddha ancestors" (S, 61).

24. In *The Great Clod*, Snyder called fossil fuels "energy slaves," that is, the new form of slavery by which we violently commandeer the power to *dominate* our place without regard to what it would otherwise have sustained. It is easy to appreciate the correlation between overpopulation, ecological degradation, and the ascendency of fossil fuels (the illusion of cheap energy and fertilizers) after World War II. Or as Snyder put it, the era of "energy slaves" "throws a whole society off keel into excess, confusion, and addiction" (GC, 28).

25. *Dōgen's* Pure Standards for the Zen Community*: A Translation of* Eihei Shingi, trans. Taigen Daniel Leighton and Shōhaku OKUMURA, ed. Taigen Daniel Leighton (1996), 38. Henceforth DPS. See also *Nothing is Hidden: Essays on Zen Master Dōgen's* Instructions for the Cook, ed. Jisho Warner, Shōhaku OKUMURA, John McRae, and Taigen Daniel Leighton (2001). I also benefited from the translation of *Tenzo Kyōkun* therein by Griffith Foulk.

26. As Edward Espe Brown, the celebrated *tenzo* of the San Francisco Zen Center, put it: "One shifts out of the mind-world of 'What's in it for me?' into the world of mutual interdependence and interconnectedness. And this is not simply something to talk about but something to be done" (DPS, xiv). Brown and the *Tenzo Kyōkun* are the focus of Doris Dörrie's wonderful film, *How to Cook Your Life* (2007).

Chapter 2
Geology (Poetic Word)

1. Some parts of this chapter appeared in a much different form in "Never Paint What Cannot Be Painted: Master Dōgen and the Zen of the Brush," *Diaphany: A Journal & Nocturne*, vol. 1, ed. Aaron Cheak, Sabrina dalla Valle, and Jennifer Zahrt (2015), 38–65.

2. *The Heart of Dōgen's Shōbōgenzō*, trans. Norman Waddell and Masao ABE (2002). Henceforth HDS.

3. Gary Snyder, "On the Road with D. T. Suzuki," *A Zen Life: D. T. Suzuki Remembered*, ed. Masao ABE (1986), 208.

4. Ibid.

5. See Olaf Pedersen, *The Book of Nature* (1992).

6. When asked what he feared most, Snyder replied "that the diversity and richness of the gene pool will be destroyed" (TI, 103).

7. That "there is nothing outside the text [*il n'ya pas de hors texte*]" is a position attributed to Derrida, although in so doing, it both misquotes and misreads him. That being said, the academic triumph of this misreading has wreaked havoc. Given that it is always interpreted, the Wild nonetheless retains a contesting element of sovereignty and alterity. See Jacques Derrida, *Limited Inc* (1988), 144. What is at stake for Snyder in this respect was first articulated by the California poet Robinson Jeffers in the preface to *The Double Axe* (1948) as "a certain philosophical attitude, which might be called Inhumanism, a shifting of emphasis and significance from man to not-man; the rejection of human solipsism and recognition of the transhuman magnificence. It seems time that our race began to think as an adult does, rather than like an egocentric baby or insane person. This manner of thought and feeling is neither misanthropic nor pessimist, though two or three people have said so and may again. It involves no falsehoods, and is a means of maintaining sanity in slippery times; it has objective truth and human value. It offers a reasonable detachment as rule of conduct, instead of love, hate and envy. It neutralizes fanaticism and wild hopes; but it provides magnificence for the religious instinct, and satisfies our need to admire greatness and rejoice in beauty" (vii).

8. Since Snyder refers to this key painting in his poem by the Wade-Giles transcription, I have here retained it throughout.

9. The critical text for this painting remains Sherman E. Lee and Wen Fong, *Streams and Mountains Without End*, second, revised edition (1967). This was also Snyder's source for the nine colophons.

10. Anthony Hunt, *Genesis, Structure, and Meaning in Gary Snyder's* Mountains and Rivers Without End (2004), 61. I would like to express my gratitude to Professor Hunt for this indispensable volume, an invaluable companion to Snyder's magnum opus. See also his helpful essay "Singing The Dyads: The Chinese Landscape Scroll and Gary Snyder's *Mountains and Rivers Without End*," *Journal of Modern Literature* 23.1 (Fall 1999), 7–34.

11. Mark Elvin, *The Retreat of the Elephants: An Environmental History of China* (2004), 9. Henceforth RE.

12. Snyder uses the Wades-Giles transcription: Hsieh Ling-yün.

13. "'Wild' in China," *"The Great Clod" Project*, excerpted in GSR, 288. "The Chinese and Japanese traditions carry within them the most sensitive, mind-deepening poetry of the natural world ever written by civilized people. Because these poets were men and women who dealt with budgets, taxes, penal systems, and the overthrow of governments, they had a heart-wrenching grasp of the contradictions that confront those who love the natural world and are yet tied to the civilized. This must be one reason why Chinese poetry is so widely appreciated by contemporary Occidentals" (GSR, 293).

14. The poem is called "[I Saw Myself]" and it is from his *Hermit Poems*: "I saw myself / a ring of bone / in the clear stream / of all of it / and vowed, / always to be open to it / that all of it / might flow through / and then heard / "ring of bone" where / ring is what a / bell does." Lew Welch, *Ring of Bone: Collected Poems of Lew Welch*

(2012), 91. Apropos of chapter 5, Snyder also admired Welch as "one of the few who saw the beauty of that ecstatic Mutual Offering called the Food Chain" (14).

15. Quoted in Patrick D. Murphy, *A Place for Wayfaring: The Poetry and Prose of Gary Snyder* (2000), 16.

16. See also Gary Snyder and Tom Killion, *Tamalpais Walking: Poetry, History, and Prints* (2009).

17. Susan Bush, "Yet Again 'Streams and Mountains Without End,'" *Artibus Asiae* XLVIII, 3/4 (1987), 197–223.

18. Snyder: "There are other ways to be taught about that state of mind than reading philosophical texts: the underlying tone in good Chinese poetry, or what is glimmering behind the surface in a Chinese Sung Dynasty landscape painting . . . is that same message about a way to *be*, that is not explicable by philosophy" (RW, 97).

19. Since Gary Snyder uses the Wade-Giles transcription throughout his poetic citations of the hand scroll, I retain them to avoid confusion.

20. I find great beauty in Snyder's desire to add a colophon to a painting that he does not own, especially given the implication of our mania for property in the ecological crisis.

21. The excessive concern with emptiness is the nihilistic and pernicious Zen *śūnyatā*-sickness (Jp. *kūbyō*), as if one were evacuating the concrete and making some kind of headlong descent into pure—that is, merely abstract—emptiness. Snyder learned this early on: "I might be misunderstanding the *Gita* in some ways, but there is a tendency in Hinduism to go out to a mind-breaking absolute point of seeing only that side of all things being impermanent, all things being illusory, and all things ultimately returning to Shiva, or the all devouring mouth of Krishna, which can be an excuse for having no responsibility to anything on your own plane. The Mahayana Buddhists think one step beyond that, that is to say, beyond the ultimate void is *this*" (RW, 20–21). Emptiness (*śūnyatā*) does not void the world so that it no longer matters. Rather, how it matters now for the first time really matters. Because of *śūnyatā* "weeds are precious, mice are precious" (RW, 21).

22. Leonard M. Scigaj, "Dōgen's Boat, Fan and Rice Cake: Realization and Artifice in Snyder's *Mountains and Rivers Without End*, "Gary Snyder: An International Perspective," special issue, ed. Patrick D. Murphy, *Studies in the Humanities* 26.1–2 (1999), 127.

23. See Steven Heine's valuable book, *The Zen Poetry of Dōgen: Verses from the Mountain of Eternal Peace* (1997).

24. NISHITANI Keiji, *Religion and Nothingness*, trans. Jan van Bragt (1982), 5. Henceforth RN.

25. For more on Schelling's critical relationship to Spinoza, see chapters 2 and 3 of my *The Conspiracy of Life: Meditations on Schelling and His Time* (2003).

26. Gudo NISHIJIMA and Chodo Cross translate *dōtoku* as "expressing the truth," "saying what one has got," or "speaking attainment." "*Dōtoku* [Expressing the

Truth]," *Master Dōgen's Shōbōgenzō*, book 2, trans. Gudo Nishijima and Chodo Cross (Dōgen Saṅgha, 1996), 229–234.

27. "Very generally, *upāya* refers to the different pedagogical styles, meditation techniques, and religious practices that help people overcome attachments, and to the ways in which Buddhism is communicated to others . . . 'skillful means' arises from the idea that wisdom is embodied in how one responds to others rather than an abstract conception of the world, and reflects an ongoing concern with the soteriological effectiveness of the Buddhist teachings." John W. Schroeder, *Skillful Means: The Heart of Buddhist Compassion* (2001), 3.

28. *Scripture of the Lotus Blossom of the Fine Dharma*, trans. Leon Hurvitz (1976), 59. Henceforth LS.

29. Hence Snyder clearly distinguishes "between visions that liberate and visions that enslave, myths that liberate and myths that do not" (NH, 20).

30. Snyder wrote the foreword to William LaFleur's early translation of Saigyō, *Mirror for the Moon* (1978), ix–xi. Snyder admires the manner of Saigyō's embrace of the moon [the Buddhist symbol of "perfect and complete enlightenment"]: "But Saigyō takes the moon into his mind and out again, it is an opening into another way of seeing this universe in all its space and with its beautiful fragile little creatures" (x).

31. William R. LaFleur, *The Karma of Words: Buddhism and the Literary Arts in Medieval Japan* (1983), 87.

32. Taigen Dan Leighton, *Visions of Awakening Space and Time: Dōgen and the Lotus Sutra* (2007), 29.

33. Quoted in Leighton, 30.

34. Wassily Kandinsky, "On the Question of Form," *The Blaue Reiter Almanac*, ed. Wassily Kandinsky and Franz Marc, trans. Klaus Lankheit (1974), 149. Henceforth QF.

35. See, for example, *Plasticity at the Dusk of Writing*, trans. Carolyn Shread (2010).

36. Marcel Franciscono, *Paul Klee: His Work and Thought* (1991), 4–5.

37. Quoted in Franciscono, 331–332. Translation of this part of the passage is my own.

38. Paul Klee, *Das bildnerische Denken* (1956), 169. "Form ist also nirgends und niemals als Erledigung, als Resultat, als Ende zu betrachten, sondern als Genesis, als Werden, als Wesen. Form als Erscheinung aber ist ein böses, gefährliches Gespenst."

39. Nishitani Keiji, "The I-Thou Relation in Zen Buddhism," trans. N. A. Waddell, *The Buddha Eye: An Anthology of the Kyoto School* (1982), 58. For more on the Kyoto School and the problem of art, see my "Truly Nothing: The Kyoto School and Art," *Japanese and Continental Philosophy: Conversations with the Kyoto School*, edited by Bret W. Davis, Brian Schroeder, and Jason M. Wirth (2011), 286–304.

40. *Kū*, 空, as we have seen, can be read as either sky or emptiness; see also MR, 162.

41. I am aware that I am transpositioning the visual and the auditory (hearing what one cannot see and seeing what one cannot hear). My motivation for this chiefly stems from Dōgen, as becomes apparent in the third section of this chapter.

42. NISHITANI Keiji, "Emptiness and Sameness," *Modern Japanese Aesthetics: A Reader*, trans and ed. Michele Marra (1999), 214. Henceforth ES. Marra notes that *soku* also denotes "namely," "=," "that is," "qua," "in other words," and "is" (ES, 179).

43. The four-line gatha in the original: "The body is the tree of enlightenment, / The mind is like a bright mirror's stand. / Time after time polish it diligently / So that no dust can collect." Translated by Stephen Addiss, *Zen Sourcebook: Traditional Documents from China, Korea, and Japan*, ed. Stephen Addiss, with Stanley Lombardo and Judith Roitman (2008), 23. Henceforth ZS.

44. Huineng's *gatha* reads: "Enlightenment is not a tree, / The bright mirror has no stand; Originally there is not one thing / What place could there be for dust" (ZS, 25)?

45. Evan Thompson, *Waking, Dreaming, Being: Self and Consciousness in Neuroscience, Meditation, and Philosophy* (2015), 122.

46. Ibid., 159.

47. Robert Hass, "Proceeding by Clues: Reading Mountains and Rivers Without End," in *A Sense of the Whole: Reading Gary Snyder's* Mountains and Rivers Without End, ed. Mark Gonnerman (2015), 198.

48. David Abram, "Gary Snyder and the Renewal of Oral Culture," in *A Sense of the Whole: Reading Gary Snyder's* Mountains and Rivers Without End, ed. Mark Gonnerman (2015), 94.

49. "I suspect that primary peoples all know that their myths are somehow 'made up.' They do not take them literally and at the same time they hold the stories very dear. Only upon being invaded by history and whipsawed by alien values do a people begin to declare that their myths are 'literally true'" (PW, 120–121).

50. See *The Vimalakīrti Sūtra*, trans. Burton Watson (1997), 90–92.

51. Ibid., 91.

Chapter 3
Place (Land and Sea, Earth and Sky)

1. Snyder to Paul Geneson in 1976: "Northern California, Oregon and Washington are where I feel most at home. On the west slope. Plus the mountains" (RW, 59).

2. Carl Bielefeldt, "Buddhism in *Mountains and Rivers Without End*," in *A Sense of the Whole: Reading Gary Snyder's* Mountains and Rivers Without End, ed. Mark Gonnerman (2015), 232. Xuanzang's pilgrimage along the Silk Road was the inspiration for the Ming Dynasty classic *Journey to the West*. In addition to securing and translating 657 sūtras including the *Mahāprajñāpāramitā Sūtra*, he was also the author of *The Great Tang Dynasty Record of the Western Regions*.

3. "An ethical life is one that is mindful, mannerly, and has style. Of all moral failings and flaws of character, the worst is stinginess of thought, which includes meanness in all its forms. Rudeness in thought or deed toward others, toward nature, reduces the chances of conviviality and interspecies communication, which are essential to physical and spiritual survival" (PW, 22).

4. Charles Olson, *Call Me Ishmael* (1947) (1997), 14. Henceforth CMI.

5. Because there are so many editions of *Moby-Dick*, citations of the novel are by chapter number and title. We employed the critical edition established in the Northwestern-Newberry Edition of *The Writings of Herman Melville*, vol. 6, ed. Harrison Hayford, Hershel Parker, and G. Thomas Tanselle (1988).

6. Gilles Deleuze and Claire Parnet, *Dialogues*, trans. Hugh Tomlinson and Barbara Habberjam (1987), 42.

7. *Distant Neighbors: The Selected Letters of Wendell Berry and Gary Snyder*, ed. Chad Wriglesworth (2014), 73. As we noted before, Snyder is likely alluding to *Genjō Kōan*: "To carry the self forward and illuminate myriad things is delusion. That myriad things come forth and illuminate the self is awakening" ("Actualizing the Fundamental Point," S, 29). The "myriad" or "ten thousand" things is shorthand to say each and every thing.

8. F. W. J. Schelling, *Über das Wesen der menschlichen Freiheit* (1809), ed. Thomas Buchheim (1997), 53. In the standard notation, this passage occurs at I/7, 383.

9. Kant makes this claim in a footnote in section 49 of the *Kritik der Urteilskraft* (*Von den Vermögen des Gemüts*). *Kritik der Urteilskraft* (1790), ed. Karl Vorländer (1990), 171.

10. Hence the 1964 Wilderness Act stipulates that "a wilderness, in contrast with those areas where man and his own works dominate the landscape, is hereby recognized as an area where the earth and its community of life are untrammeled by man, where man himself is a visitor who does not remain." The Act in itself is inherently contradictory: how can wilderness be pristine if comes into being through a congressional act? For a provocative study of this, see Margret Grebowicz. *The National Park to Come* (2015). The classic critique of the fantasy of wilderness as the pristine remains William Cronon, "The Trouble with Wilderness; or, Getting Back to the Wrong Nature," *Environmental History* 1 (1996), 7–28.

11. The great English language Dōgen scholar Steven Heine characterizes Dōgen's extraordinary style by noting that it is "characterized by a continual effort to express the inexpressible by perfecting imperfectable speech through the creative use of wordplay, neologism, and lyricism, as well as the recasting of traditional expressions." *The Zen Poetry of Dōgen: Verses from the Mountain of Eternal Peace* (1997), 67.

12. "We know the term *imperialism*—Dasmann's concept of 'biosphere cultures' helps us realize that biological exploitation is a critical part of imperialism, too: the species made extinct, the clear-cut forests" (PS, 187).

13. Nonetheless, Snyder reflects: "with the rise of the State, the scale of the destructiveness and malevolence of warfare makes a huge leap" (PW, 45).

Chapter 4
Bears (The Many Palaces of the Earth)

1. *Wo(men) and Bears: The Gifts of Nature, Culture and Gender Revisited*, ed. Kaarina Kailo (2008), 12. Henceforth WB.

2. A summary of their report and other documents can be found at: http://www.ipcc.ch/

3. See Elizabeth Kolbert, *The Sixth Extinction: An Unnatural History* (2014).

4. Arthur Schopenhauer, "On the Basis of Morals," in *The Two Fundamental Problems of Ethics*, trans. David E. Cartwright and Edward E. Erdmann (2010), 173. Henceforth BM.

5. Hallowell's dissertation was published as *Bear Ceremonialism in the Northern Hemisphere*, *American Anthropologist*, 28.1 (January–March, 1926), 1–175. The phrase "intercontinental analogies" appears on p. 163. Hallowell argues that the early human relationship to bears was not "*exclusively* utilitarian" (4) but rather characterized by "astonishing artistic performances" (4). He also argues for some discernible continuity—despite geographic variations—among ceremonial ways of hunting, feasting, and otherwise venerating bears. "In short, I think it more likely that a bear cult was one of the characteristic features of an ancient Boreal culture, Old World in origin and closely associated with the pursuit of the reindeer. Later, it became intercontinental in scope, extending from Labrador to Lapland. As this culture spread, due perhaps to the necessity of following the migrations of the animal which was the chief source of subsistence, its original traits, including a veneration of the bear and simple rites connected with hunting the animal, became more widely diffused and radically modified in the course of time. This hypothesis would account, it seems to me, for the ostensible differences in the customs described, as well as for the peculiar underlying trends and similarities observed" (161–162). Hallowell concedes that evidence suggests that bear ceremonialism could even have gone back to "some Paleolithic people" (161–162n696).

6. Michel Pastoureau, *The Bear: History of a Fallen King*, trans. George Holoch (2011), 1. Henceforth BH.

7. Friedrich Nietzsche, *Kritische Studienausgabe*, ed. Giorgio Colli and Mazzino Montinari (1980), vol. 6, 99. Henceforth KSA, followed by volume number and then page number. Nietzsche in *Beyond Good and Evil* (aphorism 289) also identified himself with a "cave bear" (KSA 5, 234).

8. See essay one, aphorism eleven of the *Genealogie* where the "blonde beast" is associated not with blonde-haired Teutons, but rather with the leonine "hidden ground" of Roman, Arabic, Germanic, Viking, Homeric, even Japanese, nonmoral values (KSA 5, 275). The lion refers to the second of the three metamorphoses in

the first book of *Zarathustra*. See also Paul Loeb, "Zarathustra's Laughing Lions," *A Nietzschean Bestiary: Becoming Animal Beyond Docile and Brutal*, ed. Christa Davis Acampora and Ralph R. Acampora (2004), 121–139.

9. William Faulkner, "The Bear," in *Go Down, Moses, Novels 1942–1954*, ed. Joseph Blotner and Noel Polk (1994). Henceforth B.

10. In chapter 5 we learn that the "the perfect condition of slavery" is "but the state of war continued, between a lawful conqueror and a captive."

11. James A. Rawley with Stephen D. Behrendt, *The Transatlantic Slave Trade: A History*, revised edition (2005), 133. "John Locke, philosopher of liberty and equality, was a subscriber." Charles W. Mills, taken by the "astonishing inconsistency" that Locke could have insisted on self-ownership and individual liberty, yet financially supported the slave trade and "assisted in writing the slave constitution of Carolina," wondered if Locke "saw blacks as not fully human and thus subject to a different set of normative rules." Charles W. Mills, *The Racial Contract* (1997), 168. My discussion of article 110 of the *Fundamental Constitutions of Carolina* derives from David Armitage, "John Locke, Carolina, and the *Two Treatises of Government*," *Political Theory* 32.5 (October 2004), 602–627. Armitage reports that Locke personally augmented article 110 by inserting the phrase "power and" so that it read "absolute [power and] Authority over his negro slaves" (609). Slaves, like indigenous peoples, would be granted religious toleration, but this would not exempt them "from that civil dominion his Master hath over him" (609).

12. Edouard Glissant, *Faulkner, Mississippi*, trans. Barbara Lewis and Thomas C. Spear (1999), 121.

13. Catherine McClellan, *The Girl Who Married the Bear: A Masterpiece of Indian Oral Tradition* (1970).

14. David Foster Wallace, *This Is Water: Some Thoughts, Delivered on a Significant Occasion, about Living a Compassionate Life* (2009), 3–4.

Chapter 5
The Great Potlatch

1. Gary Snyder, "Foreword," in Lew Welch, *Ring of Bone: Collected Poems* (2012), 14.

2. "Re-Inhabitation," OW, 65.

3. F. W. J. Schelling, *Über das Wesen der menschlichen Freiheit* (1809), ed. Thomas Buchheim (1997), 28–29. In the standard notation, this passage occurs at I/7, 356–357.

4. Bruno Latour, *We Have Never Been Modern*, trans. Catherine Porter (1993), 27. Henceforth WNM.

5. "And if we talk about evolution of consciousness, we also have to talk about evolution of bodies, which takes place by that sharing of energies, passing it back

and forth, which is done by literally eating each other. And that's what communion is" (RW, 89). Communion is not only the ancient manners of showing respect for consumption and for hunting, but also in the giving of one's body back to the Earth as in the sky burials of the Tibetan plateau or by all of the microscopic creatures that expedite our putrefaction when we die. Perhaps traces of this insight are also discernible in the "communion" of the Christian Eucharist? Snyder: "A key transaction in natural systems is energy exchange, which includes the food chains and the food webs, and this means that many living beings live by eating other beings. Our bodies—or the energy they represent—are thus continually passed around. We are all guests at the feast, and we are also the meal! All of biological nature can be seen as an enormous *puja*, a ceremony of offering and sharing" (PS, 76–77).

6. On Snyder's pursuit of a Turtle Island counterculture, see Timothy Gray, *Gary Snyder and the Pacific Rim: Creating Countercultural Community* (2006).

7. Leslie Marmon Silko, "An Old-Time Indian Attack Conducted in Two Parts," *Yardbird Reader* 5 (1976), 77–85. Murphy notes, however, "that letters written by Silko to Snyder from the early-1970's through 1977, collected in the Gary Snyder Archives at UC Davis, include no criticism by Silko of Snyder's work." Patrick D. Murphy, *A Place for Wayfaring: The Poetry and Prose of Gary Snyder* (2000), 218n43. Snyder defends Silko's "shivery novel *Ceremony*" (PS, 244). For a strong and convincing defense of Snyder in this respect, see Tim Dean, "The Other Voice: Cultural Imperialism and Poetic Impersonality in Gary Snyder's *Mountains and Rivers Without End*," *Contemporary Literature* 41.3 (Fall 2000), 462–494.

8. Snyder told Jonathan White in 1994 that "I long ago learned to control my desire to go to certain native ceremonies—out of respect for them, actually. I felt that it was better that they happened without me intruding, and that I could enjoy them from afar. I feel that way about grizzly bears, that their space should be their own. And yet I would love to hang out with them, ideally. But maybe one of the ways that we hang out with them is in stories, since it is not a good idea to do it too literally." Quoted in Timothy Gray, *Gary Snyder and the Pacific Rim: Creating Countercultural Community* (2006), 277.

9. Snyder tells us that Wovoka's famous big hat was said to contain "all the wildlife and native homelands of the pre-white world" (MR, 165). In the famous "Messiah Letter" (1890) preserved by James Mooney, we are told in his freely rendered version that "the dead are still alive again. I do not know when they will be here; maybe this fall or in the spring. When the time comes there will be no more sickness and everyone will be young again. Do not refuse to work for the whites and do not make any trouble with them until you leave them. When the earth shakes [at the coming of the new world] do not be afraid. It will not hurt you." Michael Hittman, *Wovoka and the Ghost Dance*, expanded ed., ed. Don Lynch (1997), 298. Wovoka's Nanisśaanah spread widely through indigenous communities all over Turtle Island and it was a performance of the Ghost Dance by the Lakota Sioux that precipitated the infamous massacre at Wounded Knee.

10. Snyder: "This doesn't mean some return to a primitive lifestyle or utopian provincialism; it simply implies an engagement with community and a search for the sustainable sophisticated mix of economic practices that would enable people to live regionally and yet learn from and contribute to a planetary society. . . . Such people are, regardless of national or ethnic backgrounds, in the process of becoming something deeper than 'American (or Mexican or Canadian) citizens'—they are becoming natives of Turtle Island" (PS, 247).

11. Snyder has made this point many times. For example, in 1976 at Swarthmore College, Snyder said that "I feel that mythology and folklore are the *kōans* of humanity and that all of humanity has that as its store of feelings to deeply return to over and over again, and to make one more leap into a very sizable community" (RW, 84).

12. The entry for "pot-latch" in T. N. Hibben's *The Dictionary of the Chinook Jargon or Indian Trade Language of the North Pacific Coast* (1889) reads: "A gift; to give. *Cultus* potlatch, a present or free gift."

13. Robert Bringhurst, *A Story Sharp as a Knife* (1999), 447n10. Henceforth SSK.

14. Douglas Cole, "The History of the Kwakiutl Potlatch," *Chiefly Feasts: The Enduring Kwakiutl Potlatch*, ed. Aldona Jonaitis (1991), 140.

15. Georges Bataille, *The Accursed Share*, vol. 1, trans. Robert Hurley (1988), 69. Henceforth AS.

Chapter 6
Seeds of Earth Democracy

1. This is the Buddha as the *Bhaiṣajya-guru-vaiḍūrya-prabhā-rāja*, the King or *Rāja* of the medicine master and lapis lazuli light.

2. Charles Molesworth, *Gary Snyder's Vision: Poetry and the Real Work* (1983), 128.

3. "Poetry within the civilized area of history is the fragmented attempt to recreate a 'healing song' aspect of the shaman's practice" (RW, 175).

4. This phrase comes from the essay, "Earth Day and the War Against the Imagination," PS, 56–64.

5. NISHITANI Keiji, *Religion and Nothingness*, trans. Jan van Bragt (1982), 21.

6. "Buddha Lands," *The Vimalakirti Sūtra*, trans. Burton Watson (1997), 29.

7. *Distant Neighbors: The Selected Letters of Wendell Berry and Gary Snyder*, ed. Chad Wriglesworth (2014), 73. To reiterate, Snyder is likely alluding to *Genjō Kōan*: "To carry the self forward and illuminate myriad things is delusion. That myriad things come forth and illuminate the self is awakening" ("Actualizing the Fundamental Point," S, 29).

8. Vandana Shiva, *Earth Democracy: Justice, Sustainability, and Peace* (2005), 2. Henceforth ED.

9. Karma Ura, Sabina Alkire, Tshoki Zangmo, Karma Wangdi, *A Short Guide to Gross National Happiness Index* (2012), 6. Henceforth GNH.

10. Ignacio Ellacuría, *Essays on History, Liberation, and Salvation*, ed. Michael E. Lee (2013), 29. Henceforth ELS.

11. Quoted in Patrick D. Murphy, *A Place for Wayfaring: The Poetry and Prose of Gary Snyder* (2000), 14.

12. "Even as we acknowledge the basic truth that every one of us lives by causing some harm, we can consciously amend our behavior to reduce the amount of practical damage we might do, without being drawn into needless feelings of guilt" (PS, 79).

13. Patrick D. Murphy, *Understanding Gary Snyder* (1992), 35. See also Barnhill, esp. 202–204. "But, for the traditional shaman the ultimate goal is not one's personal communication with the transhuman. It is healing. In traditional shamanistic societies, personal illness is seen not simply as a function of a body but in the person's relationship with the larger society of beings" (Barnhill, 204).

14. Eric Todd Smith rightly concludes that Snyder asks us "to think more deeply about the particulars of place and to embrace the pluralistic emptiness of many places. . . . No place is purer or more real than any other. Each has its own suchness. All are ultimately impermanent." *Reading Gary Snyder's* Mountains and Rivers Without End (2000), 44–45. When Ursula Heise lumps Snyder into the camp of those who relegate the "local" to "a miniature version of the globe and indeed the cosmos" (38) because he "sees the transnational and global realms as supplements to locally based identities" (44), I think that she does not appreciate the force and nature of nondual thinking. There is no local without the earth and no earth without the local. To separate one from the other is to render both as abstractions. Snyder is not bemused by the lure of the local. See Ursula Heise, *Sense of Place and Sense of Planet: The Environmental Imagination of the Global* (2008).

15. Quoted in *A Sense of the Whole: Reading Gary Snyder's* Mountains and Rivers Without End, ed. Mark Gonnerman (2015), 258.

Bibliography

ABE Masao. *A Study of Dōgen: His Philosophy and Religion*. Edited by Steven Heine. Albany: State University of New York Press, 1992.

———. *Zen and Western Thought*. Edited by William R. LaFleur. Honolulu: University of Hawai'i Press, 1985.

Addiss, Stephen, with Stanley Lombardo and Judith Roitman, eds. and trans. *Zen Sourcebook: Traditional Documents from China, Korea, and Japan*. Indianapolis: Hackett, 2008.

Altieri, Charles. *Enlarging the Temple: New Directions in American Poetry During the 1960s*. Lewisburg, PA: Bucknell University Press, 1979.

———. "Gary Snyder's Lyric Poetry: Dialectic as Ecology." In: *Far Point*, vol. 4 (1970), 55–65.

———. "Gary Snyder's *Turtle Island*: The Problem of Reconciling the Roles of Seer and Prophet." In: *Boundary 2: An International Journal of Literature and Culture*, 4.3 (Spring 1976), 761–777.

Armitage, David. "John Locke, Carolina, and the *Two Treatises of Government*." In: *Political Theory* 32.5 (October 2004), 602–627.

Banerjee, Neela, and Lisa Song and David Hasemyer. "Exxon: The Road not Taken: Exxon's Own Research Confirmed Fossil Fuels' Role in Global Warming Decades Ago." In: *Inside Climate News* (September 16, 2015).

Barnhill, David Landis. "An Interwoven World: Gary Snyder's Cultural Ecosystem." In: *Worldviews: Environment, Culture, and Religion* 6.2 (Fall 2002), 111–144.

———. "Great Earth *Saṅgha*: Gary Snyder's View of Nature as Community." In: *Buddhism and Ecology: The Interconnection of Dharma and Deeds*. Cambridge, MA: Harvard University Press, 1998, 187–217.

———, and Roger S. Gottlieb, eds. *Deep Ecology and World Religions: New Essays on Sacred Ground*. Albany: State University of New York Press, 2001.

Bataille, Georges. *The Accursed Share*, vol. 1. Translated by Robert Hurley. New York: Zone Books, 1988.

Bergoglio, Jorge Mario [Pope Francis]. *Encyclical Letter "Laudato Si'" of the Holy Father Francis: On Care for Our Common Home*. Vatican City: Vatican Press, 2015.

Bodiford, William M. *Sōtō Zen in Medieval Japan*. Honolulu: University Press of Hawai'i, 1993.

Bringhurst, Robert. *A Story as Sharp as a Knife: The Classical Haida Mythtellers and Their World*. Lincoln: University of Nebraska Press, 1999.

Bush, Susan. "Yet Again 'Streams and Mountains Without End.'" In: *Artibus Asiae* XLVIII, 3/4 (1987), 197–223.

Callicott, J. Baird, and Roger T. Ames, eds. *Nature in Asian Traditions of Thought: Essays in Environmental Philosophy*. Albany: *State University of New Press, 1989*.

Celan, Paul. "The Meridian." In: *Selected Poems and Prose of Paul Celan*. Translated by John Felstiner. New York and London: Norton, 2001.

Cole, Douglas. "The History of the Kwakiutl Potlatch." In: *Chiefly Feasts: The Enduring Kwakiutl Potlatch*. Edited by Aldona Jonaitis. Seattle: University of Washington Press, 1991.

Confucius [Kongzi]. *The Analects of Confucius: A Philosophical Translation*. Translated by Roger T. Ames and Henry Rosemont Jr. New York: Random House, 2010.

Cook, Francis H. *Hua-Yen Buddhism: The Jewel Net of Indra*. University Park and London: Pennsylvania State University Press, 1977.

Cronon, William. "The Trouble with Wilderness; or, Getting Back to the Wrong Nature." In: *Environmental History* 1 (1996), 7–28.

Curtin, Deane. "Dōgen, Deep Ecology, and the Ecological Self." In: *Environmental Philosophy in Asian Traditions of Thought*. Edited by J. Baird Callicott and James McRae. Albany: State University of New Press, 2014, 267–289.

Dasmann, Raymond F. *The Destruction of California*. New York: MacMillan, 1965.

———. *A Different Kind of Country*. New York: MacMillan, 1968.

Davis, Bret W. "The Enlightening Practice of Nonthinking: Unfolding Dōgen's 'Fukanzazengi.'" In: *Engaging Dōgen's Zen: The Philosophy of Practice as Awakening (Commentaries on Dōgen's "Shushōgi" and "Fukanzazengi")*. Edited by Jason M. Wirth, Brian Schroeder, and Bret Davis. Boston: Wisdom, 2017.

———, Brian Schroeder, and Jason M. Wirth, eds. *Japanese and Continental Philosophy: Conversations with the Kyoto School*. Bloomington: Indiana University Press, 2011.

Dean, Tim. *Gary Snyder and the American Unconscious: Inhabiting the Ground*. Palgrave MacMillan. 1991.

———. "The Other Voice: Cultural Imperialism and Poetic Impersonality in Gary Snyder's *Mountains and Rivers Without End*." In: *Contemporary Literature* 41.3 (Fall 2000), 462–494.

Deleuze, Gilles, and Claire Parnet. *Dialogues*. Translated by Hugh Tomlinson and Barbara Habberjam. New York: Columbia University Press, 1987.

Derrida, Jacques. *Limited Inc*. Evanston: Northwestern University Press, 1988.

Dōgen Eihei. *Dōgen's Extensive Record: A Translation of* Eihei Kōroku. Translated by Dan Leighton and Shōhaku OKUMURA. Boston: Wisdom, 2004.

———. *Dōgen's Manuals of Zen Meditation*. Translated by Carl Bielefeldt. Berkeley and Los Angeles: University of California Press, 1988.

———. *Dōgen's* Pure Standards for the Zen Community*: A Translation of* Eihei Shingi. Translated by Taigen Daniel Leighton and Shōhaku OKUMURA. Edited by Taigen Daniel Leighton. Albany: State University of New York Press, 1996.

———. *The Heart of Dōgen's Shōbōgenzō*. Translated by Norman Waddell and Masao ABE. Albany: State University of New York Press, 2002.

———. *Master Dōgen's Shōbōgenzō*. Four volumes. Translated by Gudō Wafu NISHIJIMA and Mike Chodo Cross. London: Windbell, 1994.

———. *Moon in a Dewdrop: Writings of Zen Master Dōgen*. Edited by Kazuaki TANAHASHI. San Francisco: North Point Press, 1985.

———. *A Primer of Sōtō Zen* [Shōbōgenzō Zuimonki]. Translated by Reihō MASUNAGA. Honolulu: University of Hawai'i Press, 1971.

———. *Treasury of the True Dharma Eye* [Shōbōgenzō]. Two volumes. Edited by Kazuaki TANAHASHI. Boston and London: Shambhala, 2010.

———. *The Wholehearted Way: A Translation of Eihei Dōgen's* Bendōwa *with Commentary by Kōshō Uchiyama Rōshi*. Translated by Shōhaku OKUMURA and Taigen Daniel Leighton. North Clarendon, VT: Tuttle, 1997.

———. *The Zen Poetry of Dōgen: Verses from the Mountain of Eternal Peace*. Translated by Steven Heine. North Clarendon, VT: Tuttle, 1997.

Edelglass, William, and Jay L. Garfield, eds. *Buddhist Philosophy: Essential Readings*. Oxford and New York: Oxford University Press, 2009.

Egan, Charles. "Poetic Insights: An Interview with Gary Snyder." In: *Poets & Writers Magazine* (May/June 1995), 68–75.

Ellacuría, Ignacio. *Essays on History, Liberation, and Salvation*. Edited by Michael E. Lee. Maryknoll, NY: Orbis, 2013.

Elvin, Mark. *Retreat of the Elephants: An Environmental History of China*. New Haven: Yale University Press, 2004.

Faulkner, William. "The Bear." In: *Go Down, Moses, Novels 1942–1954*. Edited by Joseph Blotner and Noel Polk. New York: Library of America, 1994.

The Flower Ornament Scripture: A Translation of the Avataṃsaka Sūtra. Translated by Thomas Cleary. Boston: Shambhala, 1993.

Franciscono, Marcel. *Paul Klee: His Work and Thought*. Chicago: University of Chicago Press, 1991.

Glissant, Edouard. *Faulkner, Mississippi*. Translated by Barbara Lewis and Thomas C. Spear. New York: Farrar, Straus and Giroux, 1999.

Gonnerman, Mark, ed. *A Sense of the Whole: Reading Gary Snyder's* Mountains and Rivers Without End. Berkeley: Counterpoint, 2015.

Gray, Timothy. *Gary Snyder and the Pacific Rim: Creating Countercultural Community*. Iowa City: University of Iowa Press, 2006.

Grebowicz, Margret. *The National Park to Come*. Stanford, CA: Stanford University Press, 2015.

Hallowell, Alfred Irving. *Bear Ceremonialism in the Northern Hemisphere*. In: *American Anthropologist*, 28.1 (January–March, 1926), 1–175.

Halper, Jon, ed. *Gary Snyder: Dimensions of a Life*. San Francisco: Sierra Club, 1991.

Harding, Stephan. "Gaia and Biodiversity." In: *Gaia in Turmoil: Climate Change, Biodepletion, and Earth Ethics in an Age of Crisis*. Edited by Eileen Crist and H. Bruce Rinker. Cambridge, MA: MIT Press, 2010.

Heise, Ursula. *Sense of Place and Sense of Planet: The Environmental Imagination of the Global*. Oxford: Oxford University Press, 2008.

Henning, Daniel H. *Buddhism and Deep Ecology*. Bloomington: 1st Books, 2002.

Hibben, T. N. *The Dictionary of the Chinook Jargon or Indian Trade Language of the North Pacific Coast*. Victoria, British Columbia: Hibben, 1889.

Hittman, Michael. *Wovoka and the Ghost Dance*. Expanded ed. Edited by Don Lynch. Lincoln, NE: Bison Books, 1997.

Huesemann, Michael H., and Joyce A. Huesemann. *Technofix: Why Technology Won't Save Us or the Environment*. Gabriola Island, British Columbia: New Society, 2011.

Hunt, Anthony. *Genesis, Structure, and Meaning in Gary Snyder's* Mountains and Rivers Without End. Reno: University of Nevada Press, 2004.

———. "Singing the Dyads: The Chinese Landscape Scroll and Gary Snyder's *Mountains and Rivers Without End*." In: *Journal of Modern Literature* 23.1 (1999), 7–34.

James, Simon P. *Zen Buddhism and Environmental Ethics*. New York: Ashgate, 2004.

Jeffers, Robinson. *The Double Axe and Other Poems*. New York: Random House, 1948.

Jerving, Sara, and Katie Jennings, Masako Melissa Hirsch, and Susanne Rust. "What Exxon Knew about the Earth's Melting Arctic." In: *Los Angeles Times* (October 9, 2015).

Jullien, François. *Vivre de paysage ou l'impensé de la raison*. Paris: Gallimard, 2014.

Jung, Hwa Yol, and Petee Jung, "Gary Snyder's Ecopiety." In: *Environmental History Review*, 14.3 (Autumn, 1990), 74–87.

Kailo, Kaarina, ed. *Wo(men) and Bears: The Gifts of Nature, Culture and Gender Revisited*. Toronto: Inanna, 2008.

Kandinsky, Wassily. "On the Question of Form." In: *The Blaue Reiter Almanac*. Edited by Wassily Kandinsky and Franz Marc. Translated by Klaus Lankheit. New York: Viking, 1974.

Kant, Immanuel. Kant, *Anthropology, History, and Education*. Edited and translated by Robert B. Louden and Günter Zöller. Cambridge: Cambridge University Press, 2008.

———. *Kritik der Urteilskraft* (1790). Edited by Karl Vorländer. Hamburg: Felix Meiner Verlag, 1990.

Kim, Hee-Jin. *Dōgen Kigen: Mystical Realist*. Tucson: University of Arizona Press, 1987.

———. *Dōgen on Meditation and Thinking: A Reflection on His View of Zen*. Albany: State University of New York Press, 2007.

Klee, Paul. *Das bildnerische Denken*. Basel/Stuttgart: Benno Schwabe, 1956.

Kolbert, Elizabeth. *The Sixth Extinction: An Unnatural History*. New York: Holt, 2014.

Kopf, Gereon. *Beyond Personal Identity: Dōgen, Nishida, and a Phenomenology of No-Self*. Richmond, Surrey: Curzon Press, 2001.

Kraft, Kenneth. "The Greening of Buddhist Practice." In: *CrossCurrents* 14.2 (Summer 1994), 163–180.

Kuperus, Gerard. *Ecopolitical Homelessness: Defining Place in an Unsettled World*. London and New York: Routledge, 2016.

LaFleur, William R. *The Karma of Words: Buddhism and the Literary Arts in Medieval Japan*. Berkeley: University of California Press, 1983.

———, ed. *Dōgen Studies*. Honolulu: University of Hawai'i Press, 1985.

Latour, Bruno. *We Have Never Been Modern*. Translated by Catherine Porter. Cambridge, MA: Harvard University Press, 1993.

Lee, Sherman E., and Wen Fong. *Streams and Mountains Without End*. Second, revised ed. Ascona, Switzerland: Artibus Asiae, 1967.

Leighton, Taigen Dan. *Visions of Awakening Space and Time: Dōgen and the* Lotus Sutra. Oxford and New York: Oxford University Press, 2007.

Locke, John. *Two Treatises of Government* (1689). Edited by Peter Laslett. Cambridge: Cambridge University Press, 1988.

Loeb, Paul. "Zarathustra's Laughing Lions." In: *A Nietzschean Bestiary: Becoming Animal Beyond Docile and Brutal*. Edited by Christa Davis Acampora and Ralph R. Acampora. Lanham, MD: Rowman & Littlefield, 2004, 121–139.

Malabou, Catherine. *Plasticity at the Dusk of Writing*. Translated by Carolyn Shread. New York: Columbia University Press, 2010.

Martin, Julia. "Practicing Emptiness: Gary Snyder's Playful Ecological Work." In: *Western American Literature* 27.1 (1992), 3–19.

———. "Seeing a Corner of the Sky in Gary's Snyder's *Mountains and Rivers Without End*." In: *Western American Literature* 40.1 (Spring 2005), 55–87.

Matthews, Freya. *The Ecological Self*. London and New York: Routledge, 1991.

McClellan, Catherine. *The Girl Who Married the Bear: A Masterpiece of Indian Oral Tradition*. Ottawa: National Museums of Canada, 1970.

McClintock, James I. *Nature's Kindred Spirits: Aldo Leopold, Joseph Wood Krutch, Edward Abbey, Annie Dillard, and Gary Snyder*. Madison: University of Wisconsin Press, 1994.

McRae, John R. *Seeing through Zen: Encounter, Transformation, and Genealogy in Chinese Chan Buddhism*. Berkeley: University of California Press, 2003.

Melville, Herman. *Moby-Dick, or The Whale* (1851). The Northwestern-Newberry Edition of *The Writings of Herman Melville*, vol. 6. Edited by Harrison Hayford,

Hershel Parker, and G. Thomas Tanselle. Evanston and Chicago: Northwestern University Press and the Newberry Library, 1988.

Mickey, Sam. *Whole Earth Thinking and Planetary Coexistence: Ecological Wisdom at the Intersection of Religion, Ecology, and Philosophy*. London and New York: Routledge, 2016.

Mills, Charles W. *The Racial Contract*. Ithaca: Cornell University Press, 1997.

Molesworth, Charles. *Gary Snyder's Vision: Poetry and the Real Work*. Columbia: University of Missouri Press, 1983.

Murphy, Patrick D. *A Place for Wayfaring: The Poetry and Prose of Gary Snyder*. Corvallis: Oregon State University Press, 2000.

———. *Understanding Gary Snyder*. Columbia: University of South Carolina Press, 1992.

———, ed. *Critical Essays on Gary Snyder*. Boston: Hall, 1990.

Nietzsche, Friedrich. *Kritische Studienausgabe*. Edited by Giorgio Colli and Mazzino Montinari. Munich and Berlin: Deutscher Taschenbuch Verlag and Walter de Gruyter, 1980.

NISHITANI Keiji. "Emptiness and Sameness." In: *Modern Japanese Aesthetics: A Reader*. Translated and edited by Michele Marra. Honolulu: University of Hawai'i Press, 1999.

———. "The I-Thou Relation in Zen Buddhism." Translated by N. A. Waddell. In: *The Buddha Eye: An Anthology of the Kyoto School*. New York: Crossroad, 1982.

———. *Religion and Nothingness*. Translated by Jan van Bragt. Berkeley and Los Angeles: University of California Press, 1982.

Oelschlaeger, Max. *The Idea of Wilderness: From Prehistory to the Age of Ecology*. New Haven and London: Yale University Press, 1991.

Oliver, Kelly. *Earth & World: Philosophy After the Apollo Missions*. New York: Columbia University Press, 2015.

Olson, Charles. *Call Me Ishmael* (1947). Baltimore, MD: Johns Hopkins University Press, 1997.

Pastoureau, Michel. *The Bear: History of a Fallen King*. Translated by George Holoch. Cambridge and London: Harvard University Press, 2011.

Pedersen, Olaf. *The Book of Nature*. Notre Dame, IN: University of Notre Dame Press, 1992.

Perkins, David. *A History of Modern Poetry: Modernism and After*. Cambridge, MA: Harvard University Press, 1987.

Pleasants, Ben. "Ontology of Language in the Poetry of Eliot and Snyder." In: *Tuatara*, no. 12 (1974), 53–63.

Rawley, James A. with Stephen D. Behrendt. *The Transatlantic Slave Trade: A History*. Revised ed. Lincoln: University of Nebraska Press, 2005.

Rouzer, Paul. *On Cold Mountain: A Buddhist Reading of the Hanshan Poems*. Seattle and London: University of Washington Press, 2016.

Russell, Jeff W. "Mother Gaia: A Glimpse into the Buddhist Aesthetic of Gary Snyder." In: *Japan Studies Review*, vol. 9 (2005), 123–134.
SAKAKI Nanao. *How to Live on the Planet Earth: Collected Poems*. Nobleboro, ME: Blackberry Books, 2013.
Sallis, John. *Senses of Landscape*. Evanston: Northwestern University Press, 2015.
Schelling, F. W. J. *Über das Wesen der menschlichen Freiheit* (1809). Edited by Thomas Buchheim. Hamburg: Felix Meiner Verlag, 1997.
Schopenhauer, Arthur. *The Two Fundamental Problems of Ethics*. Translated by David E. Cartwright and Edward E. Erdmann. Oxford: Oxford University Press, 2010.
Schroeder, John W. *Skillful Means: The Heart of Buddhist Compassion*. Honolulu: University of Hawai'i Press, 2001.
Schuler, Robert Jordan. *Journeys Toward the Original Mind: The Long Poems of Gary Snyder*. New York: Peter Lang, 1994.
Scigaj, Leonard M. "Dōgen's Boat, Fan and Rice Cake: Realization and Artifice in Snyder's *Mountains and Rivers Without End*." In: "Gary Snyder: An International Perspective" special issue. Edited by Patrick D. Murphy. *Studies in the Humanities* 26.1–2 (1999), 124–136.
Scripture of the Lotus Blossom of the Fine Dharma [*Saddharmapuṇḍarīka Sūtra*]. Translated by Leon Hurvitz. New York: Columbia University Press, 1976.
Shepard, Paul, and Barry Sanders. *The Sacred Paw: The Bear in Nature, Myth, and Literature*. New York: Viking, 1985.
Shiva, Vandana. *Earth Democracy: Justice, Sustainability, and Peace*. Cambridge, MA: South End Press, 2005.
Silko, Leslie Marmon. "An Old-Time Indian Attack Conducted in Two Parts." In: *Yardbird Reader* 5 (1976), 77–85.
Smith, Todd. "Place and Impermanence in Gary Snyder's *Mountains and Rivers Without End*," 112–123. In: *Studies in the Humanities*, vol. 26, no. 2 (June 1999). (Special Issue: Gary Snyder: An International Perspective)
———. *Reading Gary Snyder's* Mountains and Rivers Without End. Boise, ID: Boise State University Press, 2000.
Snyder, Gary. *Axe Handles*. San Francisco: North Point Press, 1983.
———. *The Back Country*. New York: New Directions, 1968.
———. *Back on the Fire: Essays*. Emeryville, CA: Shoemaker & Hoard, 2007.
———. *Danger on Peaks: Poems*. Emeryville, CA: Shoemaker & Hoard, 2004.
———. *Distant Neighbors: The Selected Letters of Wendell Berry and Gary Snyder*. Edited by Chad Wriglesworth. Berkeley: Counterpoint, 2014.
———. *Earth House Hold: Technical Notes and Queries to Fellow Dharma Revolutionaries*. New York: New Directions, 1969.
———. "Foreword." In: Saigyō, *Mirror for the Moon*. Edited and translated by William LaFleur. New York: New Directions, 1978, ix–xi.

———. "Foreword." In: *Zen Forest: Sayings of the Masters*. Edited by Sōiku Shigematsu. New York: Weatherhill, 1981, vii–xii.

———. *The Gary Snyder Reader: Prose, Poetry and Translations, 1952–1998*. Washington, DC: Counterpoint, 1999.

———. *The Great Clod: Notes and Memoirs on Nature and History in East Asia*. Berkeley: Counterpoint, 2016.

———. *He Who Hunted Birds in His Father's Village: The Dimensions of a Haida Myth (1951)*. Emeryville, CA: Shoemaker & Hoard, 2007.

———. *Left Out in the Rain: New Poems 1947–1985*. San Francisco: North Point Press, 1986.

———. *Mountains and Rivers without End*. Washington, DC: Counterpoint, 1996.

———. "Mountains Hidden in Mountains: Dōgen-zenji and the Mind of Ecology." In: *Dōgen Zen and Its Relevance for Our Time*. Edited by Shōhaku OKUMURA. San Francisco: Sōtō Zen Buddhism International Center, 2003, 159–172.

———. *Myths & Texts* (1960). New York: New Directions, 1978.

———. *No Nature: New and Selected Poems*. New York: Pantheon, 1992.

———. *North Pacific Lands and Waters: A Further Six Sections*. Waldron Island, WA: Brooding Heron Press, 1993.

———. *The Old Ways: Six Essays*. San Francisco: City Lights, 1977.

———. "On the Road with D. T. Suzuki." In: *A Zen Life: D. T. Suzuki Remembered*. Edited by Masao ABE. New York: Weatherhill, 1986, 207–209.

———. *Passage Through India*. Expanded edition. Emeryville, CA: Shoemaker & Hoard, 2007.

———. *A Place in Space: Ethics, Aesthetics, and Watersheds: New and Selected Prose*. Washington, DC: Counterpoint, 1995.

———. *The Practice of the Wild* (1990). Berkeley: Counterpoint, 2010.

———. *A Range of Poems*. London: Fulcrum Press, 1966

———. *The Real Work: Interviews & Talks 1964–1979*. Edited by William Scott McLean. New York: New Directions, 1980.

———. "The Rediscovery of Turtle Island." In: *Deep Ecology for the 21st Century: Readings on the Philosophy and Practice of the New Environmentalism*. Edited by George Sessions. Boston and London: Shambhala, 1995.

———. *Regarding Wave*. New York: New Directions, 1970.

———. *Riprap and Cold Mountain Poems*. San Francisco: North Point Press, 1990.

———. *This Present Moment: New Poems*. Berkeley: Counterpoint, 2015.

———. *Turtle Island*. New York: New Directions, 1974.

———, and Julia Martin. *Nobody Home: Writing, Buddhism, and Living in Places*. San Antonio, TX: Trinity University Press, 2014.

———, and Tom Killion. *Tamalpais Walking: Poetry, History, and Prints*. Berkeley, California: Heyday, 2009.

Stirling, Isabel. *Zen Pioneer: The Life and Works of Ruth Fuller Sasaki*. Emeryville, CA: Shoemaker and Hoard, 2006.

Suzuki, Daisetz T. *Essays in Zen Buddhism*, First Series. London and New York: Rider, 1926.
Tan, Joan Qionglin. *Han Shan, Chan Buddhism and Gary Snyder's Ecopoetic Way*. Eastbourne, UK, and Portland, Oregon: Sussex Academic Press, 2009.
Thompson, Evan. *Waking, Dreaming, Being: Self and Consciousness in Neuroscience, Meditation, and Philosophy*. New York: Columbia University Press, 2015.
Ura, Karma, and Sabina Alkire, Tshoki Zangmo, Karma Wangdi. *A Short Guide to the Gross National Happiness Index*. Thimpu, Bhutan: Center for Bhutan Studies, 2012.
The Vimalakīrti Sūtra [*Vimalakīrti Nirdeśa Sūtra*]. Translated by Burton Watson. New York: Columbia University Press, 1997.
Wallace, David Foster. *This Is Water: Some Thoughts, Delivered on a Significant Occasion, about Living a Compassionate Life*. New York: Little, Brown, 2009.
Warner, Jisho, Shōhaku OKUMURA, John McRae, and Taigen Daniel Leighton, eds. *Nothing is Hidden: Essays on Zen Master Dōgen's* Instructions for the Cook. New York and Tokyo: Weatherhill, 2001.
Welch, Lew. *Ring of Bone: Collected Poems*. Foreword by Gary Snyder. San Francisco: City Lights/Grey Fox, 2012.
White, Kenneth. *The Tribal Dharma: An Essay on the Work of Gary Snyder*. Dyfed, Wales: Unicorn Bookshop, 1975.
Wirth, Jason M. *The Conspiracy of Life: Meditations on Schelling and His Time*. Albany: State University of New York Press, 2003.
———. "Dōgen and the Unknown Knowns: The Practice of the Wild After the End of Nature." In: *Environmental Philosophy*, 10.1 (Spring 2013), 39–62.
———. "Never Paint What Cannot Be Painted: Master Dōgen and the Zen of the Brush." In: *Diaphany: A Journal & Nocturne*, vol. 1. Edited by Aaron Cheak, Sabrina dalla Valle, and Jennifer Zahrt. Auckland and Seattle: Rubedo Press (2015), 38–65.
———. "One Bright Pearl: On Japanese Aesthetic Expressivity." In: *The Movement of Nothingness: Trust in the Emptiness of Time*. Edited by Daniel Price and Ryan Johnson. Aurora, CO: Davies Group, 2013, 21–36.
———. "Painting Mountains and Rivers: Gary Snyder, Dōgen, and the Elemental Sutra of the Wild." In: *Research in Phenomenology*, vol. 44 (2014), 240–261.
———. *Schelling's Practice of the Wild: Time, Art, Imagination*. Albany: State University of New York Press, 2015.
———, and Brian Schroeder and Bret Davis, eds. *Engaging Dōgen's Zen: The Philosophy of Practice as Awakening (Commentaries on Dōgen's "Shushōgi" and "Fukanzazengi")*. Boston: Wisdom, 2017.
———, with Patrick Burke, eds. *Merleau-Ponty, Schelling, and the Question of Nature*. Albany: State University of New York Press, 2013.
Wright, Dale S. *Philosophical Meditations on Zen Buddhism*. Cambridge: Cambridge University Press, 1998.

Index

Abe Masao, 14–15, 51, 121n12
Abram, David, 51
Ahiṃsā (non-violence), 112–13
Anarchy, 68–69
Aristotle, 110
Avalokiteśvara. *See* Kannon
Avataṃsaka Sūtra, xviii, 36, 68
Avidyā (ignorance), 16, 43

Back country, the, 17–19, 29–30. *See also* Dao; Dharma; Wild, the
Barnhill, David Landis, xx, 132n13
Bataille, Georges, 97–99
Bears, xxiii, 8, 19, 64, 66, 71–84, 95–96, 100, 128n5, 128n7, 130n8. *See also* Smokey the Bear
Bergoglio, Jorge Mario (Pope Francis), xxi–xxii, 69, 88, 112–13; *Laudato Si'*, xxi–xxii, 69, 88, 112–13
Berry, Wendell, 100, 107, 119n19
Bhutan, 74, 109–11
Bielefeldt, Carl, 11, 57, 120n8
Bringhurst, Robert, 96
Brown, Edward Espe, 122n26
Buddha, the, xx–xxii, xxiv–xxv, 6–10, 12, 17, 21, 26, 35–39, 43–45, 48, 51, 64, 66–67, 93, 103–4, 107–8, 115, 120n4, 121n17, 131n1
Buddha Dharma, xxii, 5–7, 18, 31, 33–34, 43, 104, 120n4. *See also* Buddha Way
Buddha lands, 64, 67, 108, 110
Buddha nature, 9, 14, 29

Buddha Way, xxi–xxii, 17, 37. *See also* Buddha Dharma
Buddhism. *See* Buddha Dharma; Buddha Way

Calligraphic colophon, xxiii, xxiv, 20, 35–36. *See also* Calligraphy
Calligraphy (*shufa*), xxiii, xxiv, 20, 35–36. *See also* Calligraphic colophon
Celan, Paul, xiii, 117n3
Ch'i Shan Wu Chin (Endless Streams and Mountains), 29–30
Chōfū, xvii
Chowka, Peter Barry, 25, 118n9
Climate emergency (climate change), xv, xvii, 73, 97
Commons, 67–68, 107–108; Mind of the Commons, xx, 113; tragedy of the commons, 62, 67–68
Confucius (Kongzi), xxvi
Counterculture, xxiv, 130n6
Cronon, William, 127n10

Dao, xiv, xxvi, 5, 12, 15, 19, 23, 27, 31, 37, 42, 45–46; *Dao De Jing*, xiv. *See also* Back country, the; Dharma; Wild, the; Zhuangzi
Daokai, 12–13
Dasmann, Raymond, 66, 127n12
Davis, Bret, 118n10
Deconstruction, 28. *See also* Derrida, Jacques

Deleuze, Gilles, 59
Derrida, Jacques, 122n7. *See also*
   Deconstruction
Dharma, xiii, xx, xxii–xxiii, 6–7, 13, 15,
   18–23, 25, 27, 35–36, 38–39, 42, 44–45,
   47, 52, 57, 65, 68, 80, 92–93, 99, 104,
   121n13; Dharma eye, 20–21, 23, 25,
   38, 44, 108, 111; Dharma potlatch, 100;
   tribal Dharma, 93, 99–100. *See also*
   Back country; Buddha Dharma; Dao;
   Wild, the
Diamond Sūtra, 50
Dōgen Eihei, *Baika (Plum Blossoms)*, 3,
   39–40; *Bendōwa (Whole-hearted
   Practice of the Way)*, 15; *Bodaisatta Shi
   Shōhō (The Bodhisattva's Four Methods
   of Guidance)*, 67; Buddha to buddha
   (*yuibutsu yobutsu*; *ichibutsu-nibutsu*)
   communication, xxiv, 35; *Busshō
   (Buddha Nature)*, xxiii, 8–9, 37–38;
   Eihei Kōroku, 44; expression (*dōtoku*),
   42, 124–125n26; falling and cast-
   ing away of body and mind (*shinjin
   datsuraku*), 14, 39–40, 50; *Fukan-
   zazengi (Universally Recommended
   Instructions for Zazen)*, xviii, 118n10;
   Gabyō (Painting of a Rice Cake), 37–39;
   *Genjō Kōan (Actualizing the Funda-
   mental Point)*, 14, 17, 66, 81, 119n19,
   127n7, 131n7; *Ikka Myōju (One Bright
   Pearl)*, 26–27, 36; *Keisei Sanshoku
   (Valley Sounds, Mountain Colors)*, 6, 8,
   38; *Kesa Kudoku (Power of the Robe or
   Kesa)*, 21–22; *Kūge (Flowers in the Sky/
   Flowers of Emptiness)*, 79; oneness of
   practice and realization (*shushō-ittō*),
   26, 39, 51, 110; *Sansui-kyō (Mountains
   and Waters Sutra)*, 11–15, 30–32, 81,
   120n8, 120n9; *Semmen (Washing the
   Face)*, 8, 21, 42, 122n23; *Senjō (Cleans-
   ing)*, 21, 122n22; *shingi* (pure stan-
   dards), 21–22; 122n25; *Shoaku Makusa
   (Refrain from Unwholesome Action)*,
   15; *Shōbōgenzō Zuimonki (Treasury of
   the True Dharma Eye: Record of Things
   Heard)* 121n17; *Sokushin Zebutsu (Mind
   Right Now is Buddha)*, 9–10, 39; *Tenzo-
   kyōkun (Instructions to the Monastery
   Cook)*, 22–23, 38, 107, 122n25, 122n26;
   Uji (Time Being), 13, 21
Dostoevsky, Fyodor, xxii; *The Brothers
   Karamazov*, xxii

Earth democracy, xxiii, xxv, 28, 64, 87–88,
   91, 103–16
Earth Saṅgha, 28, 113. *See also* Saṅgha
Ecology, xviii–xx, 5, 27, 75, 84, 90–91, 100;
   cosmic ecology, xviii–xix, 120n7; depth
   ecology, 84
El Salvador, 111–12
Element (the elemental), xxii, 4–13, 29,
   32–34, 36–37, 39, 120n7
Ellacuría, Ignacio, 111–12
Elvin, Mark, 31
Emptiness (*kū*, *śūnyatā*), xx, xxii, 4, 6,
   12–13, 17, 20, 32, 35–39, 45, 47–49, 68,
   79, 81–82, 88, 103, 124n21, 125n40,
   132n14
Emptiness–sickness (*śūnyatā*–sickness,
   kūbyō), 37, 39, 47, 124n21

Faulkner, William, 75–80; *The Bear*, 75–80
Flaherty, Doug, xix, 4
Fowler, Gene, xvii, 8
Fudō Myō-ō (The Immovable Wisdom
   King), 12, 64, 116

Geneson, Paul, 109, 126n1
Ghandi, 100
Ghost Dance (Nanissáanah), 95, 115, 130n9.
   See also Wovoka
Glissant, Edouard, 79
Gramsci, Antonio, 65
Great Death, 18, 106. *See also* Nishitani Keiji
Great Doubt, 106. *See also* Nishitani Keiji
Great Earth, xiii–xiv, xx–xxv, 3–11, 14–15,
   20, 22, 27–30, 34–36, 38–39, 44, 49,
   51–52, 58–59, 64, 69, 79, 82–84, 87–88,

92, 96, 104, 106, 108, 111, 114–16, 118–19n17. *See also* Earth Saṅgha

Habito, Ruben, 108
Hakuin Ekaku, 47, 106
Hallowell, Alfred Irving, 74, 83, 128n5
Hara, xviii
Hasegawa Saburo, 34
Heidegger, Martin, 5, 16–17; *Being and Time*, 16–17
Heine, Steven, 127n11
Heise, Ursula, 132n14
Herzog, Werner, 83; *Grizzly Man*, 83
Huangbo Xiyun (Jp. Ōbaku Keun), 115
Huineng Dajian (Jp. Enō Daikan), 49
Hungry ghosts, 66, 69, 81, 92, 99, 104
Hunt, Anthony, 123n10

Imagination, xv, xx, 38, 46–49, 95, 105; war against the imagination, 105

Jeffers, Robinson, 28, 122n7; Inhumanism, 28, 122n7
Johns, Maria, 80, 83, 100

Kandinsky, Wassily, 45–46, 49
Kannon (Avalokiteśvara), 12, 108
Kant, Immanuel, 19, 61, 73
Kim, Hee-Jin, 15
Klee, Paul, 46–47
Kleśas, 104
Koda, Carole, 87
Krishna, 29, 115, 124n21

Lampe, Keith, 114
Latour, Bruno, 89–90; modern constitution, 89–90
Leopold, Aldo, xxv; land ethic, xxv
Levinas, Emmanuel, 73
Linji, xviii, 49
Locke, John, 77–78; *Second Treatise of Civil Government*, 77–78
Lotus Sutra. See *Scripture of the Lotus Blossom of the Fine Dharma*

Malabou, Catherine, 46; plasticity, 46
McClellan, Catherine, 80, 100
Melville, Herman, 58–60; *Moby-Dick*, 58–60
Mickey, Sam, 118n16
Milarepa, xxiv, 25, 87
Mills, Charles, 129n11
Mind of the Commons. *See* Commons
Money, xv, 67, 99, 119n22
Morinaga Sōkō (Kō-san), 17–18
Mountains and rivers, 3–22, 25–53, 63, 104, 113
Murphy, Patrick D., 114, 130n7

Nāgārjuna, 37–38, 50–51
Nanissáanah. *See* Ghost Dance
Natural Contract, 68
Nietzsche, Friedrich, 4, 61, 74, 128n7, 128–29n8
Nishitani Keiji, 40–41, 47–49; field of śūnyatā (*kū no ba*), 47–48; realization, 40–41
Nonduality, 4–5, 7–8, 10, 20, 118–119n17, 132n14
Nyojō Tendō. *See* Rujing Tiantong

Obata Chiura, 11
Oda Sessō Rōshi, xvii, 11, 45, 118–119n17
Olson, Charles, 58, 60

Pan-humanism, xxv
Parkes, Graham, 120n9
Pastoureau, Michel, 74–75, 77, 80, 82
Perkins, David, 3–4, 119–120n2
Place, xiii, xvi, xx, xxiii, xxv, 4, 8, 11, 13, 15, 19, 22, 25–27, 29, 33, 44, 47, 49, 51, 57–69, 81–82, 84, 87–89, 91–92, 94–95, 100, 103–8, 113–15, 118n16, 120n7, 122n24, 132n14. *See also* space; Spirits of Place
Platonism, 9–10
Potlatch, xxiii, 22, 87–101, 131n12
Poverty, xiv, 99; spiritual poverty, xv
Pratītyasamutpāda (dependent co-origination), xviii, xx–xxi, 113

Private property, 60, 77–79, 97, 106–7
Puja, 22, 87–88, 98, 129–30n5

Qingyuan Weixin, 9

Rank, 96–98; true person of no rank, xviii, 49
Rawls, John, 114
Re-inhabitation, 69, 87–88, 95–96, 114
Rujing Tiantong (Jp. Nyojō Tendō), 39–41, 43

Saigyō, 125n30
San Francisco, 105
San Francisco Renaissance, 71–72
Saṅgha, 18, 31, 114–15. *See also* Earth Saṅgha
Schelling, F.W.J., 41, 46, 61, 89, 121n12; unprethinkable (*unvordenklich*), 13, 121n12
Schopenhauer, Arthur, 73, 78–79
Scripture of the Lotus Blossom of the Fine Dharma (*The Lotus Sutra*), 43–44, 52
Schroeder, John W., 125n27
Shan-shui painting, 29–34
Shiva, Vandana, 107–8
Silko, Leslie Marmon, 94, 130n7
Sixth Great Extinction, xv, 22, 53
Slavery, 65, 67, 77–79, 122n24, 129n10
Smith, Eric Todd, 119n22
Smokey the Bear, 63–64, 71–72. *See also* Bears
Snyder, Gary, *Axe Handles,* 116; *Back on the Fire: Essays,* xiii, xv, xxi, 19, 90–91, 95, 98, 112–13; "Berry Feast," 71, 80; *Danger on Peaks: Poems,* 121n13; *Earth House Hold: Technical Notes and Queries to Fellow Dharma Revolutionaries,* 91–93, 100, 114; *The Great Clod: Notes and Memoirs on Nature and History in East Asia,* 30–31, 122n24; *The Gary Snyder Reader: Prose, Poetry, and Translations, 1952–1998,* xxiii, 16, 28, 32–33, 92, 94–95, 123n13; *He Who Hunted Birds in His Father's Village:*

The Dimensions of a Haida Myth, 96–97, 99, 101; "How Poetry Comes to Me," 51; "Is Nature Real?," 16; "Mountains Hidden in Mountains: Dōgen-zenji and the Mind of Ecology," 11, 21–22, 120n8; *Mountains and Rivers without End,* xx, xxiii–xxiv, 6–8, 10–12, 14, 17–18, 20, 25–26, 29–30, 34–37, 39, 50–53, 57, 71, 87–88, 95–96, 103, 115, 120n7, 120–21n10, 121n19, 130n9; *Nobody Home: Writing, Buddhism, and Living in Places,* xvii, 7, 19, 33, 42–43, 84, 111, 117n7, 125n29; *This Present Moment: New Poems,* 51; *A Place in Space: Ethics, Aesthetics, and Watersheds: New and Selected Prose,* xxiv–xxv, 15, 57–58, 64–69, 87–88, 105–6, 112, 114–15, 127n12, 120–30n5, 130n7, 131n10, 132n12; *The Practice of the Wild,* xiv, xvi, xx, xxiii, 18–19, 25, 30, 34, 44–45, 63, 65, 67–69, 73, 77, 81, 83–84, 90–91, 113–14, 117n4, 126n49, 127n3, 128n13; *The Real Work: Interviews & Talks 1964–1979,* xiv–xv, xvi, xviii, xix–xxi, xxiv–xvi, 4, 8, 20, 25, 27, 29, 58, 66, 71, 92, 96, 104, 106, 108–9, 111, 114, 117n4, 117n5, 118n8, 118n9, 118n13, 118n14, 118–19n17, 124n18, 124n21, 126n1, 129–30n5, 131n11, 131n3; *Smokey the Bear Sutra, The,* 63–64; *Turtle Island,* xvi, xxiii, xxv, 8, 64–65, 75, 88, 94–95, 98, 104–5, 113–14, 120n3, 122n6
Space, 58–63, 76–77, 83, 125n30. *See also* place; Spirits of Place
Spirits of Place, 95, 106–8, 110, 112, 115. *See also* place; space
Su Dongpo, 6–7
Suzuki Daisetz Teitarō, 9, 27, 120n5

Tan, Joan Qionglin, 120n6
Tanahashi Kazuaki, 11, 40
Tārā, 7, 10–11, 34, 36, 39, 42, 52–53, 71, 84, 88, 95, 103, 114
Thompson, Evan, 50–51

Turtle Island, xvii–xiv, 4–5, 29, 32–33, 52, 57–59, 64, 69, 88, 91, 94–96, 103, 105–7, 111, 114–16, 120n3, 130n6, 130n9, 131n10

Upāya (skillful means), xxiii, 4, 18, 37–40, 43–45, 49, 51–52, 84, 95, 101, 115, 125n27

Vimalakīrti Sūtra, 52, 107, 115

Wallace, David Foster, 81–82
Welch, Lew, 123–24n14
White, Jonathan, 130n8
Wild, The, xvii, xxii, 3, 5–6, 10–11, 13, 15–21, 26–34, 39–42, 45, 51, 58, 63, 65–66, 68–69, 89, 100, 104, 113, 117n4, 119–20n2, 123n7. *See also* Back country; Dao; Dharma
Wilderness Act (1964), 127n10

William of Auvergne, 82–83
Wovoka, 29, 57, 95, 115, 130n9. *See also* Ghost Dance

Xuansha Shibei, 26–27
Xuanzang, 57, 126n2

Yamabushi, 64, 71, 82
Yamazato Katsunori, 18

Zazen (sitting Zen), xviii, 8, 21–22, 92, 96, 118n17. *See also* Zen
Zeami, 12, 120–21n10; *Yamaba* (*Old Mountain Woman*), 12, 120–121n10
Zen, xiv, xvii–xviii, xix, xxvi, 3–4, 8–9, 11, 14–15, 18, 21–22, 25, 29, 32–34, 37, 43–45, 47, 49, 66, 80, 87–88, 92–93, 105–7, 110, 116, 118n9, 118–19n17, 120n5, 122n26, 124n21. *See also* Zazen
Zhuangzi, 30, 45–46

www.ingramcontent.com/pod-product-compliance
Ingram Content Group UK Ltd.
Pitfield, Milton Keynes, MK11 3LW, UK
UKHW021846140426
5217IPUK00022B/1622